*To:*

_____

*From:*

_____

*Date:*

_____

# GOD'S
## WISDOM
### for Your Life

BARBOUR
PUBLISHING

© 2011 by Barbour Publishing, Inc.

Written and compiled by Pamela L. McQuade

ISBN 978-1-61626-464-2

Published by Barbour Publishing, Inc., P.O. Box 719, Uhrichsville, Ohio 44683, www.barbourbooks.com

*Our mission is to publish and distribute inspirational products offering exceptional value and biblical encouragement to the masses.*

Member of the
Evangelical Christian
Publishers Association

Printed in the United States of America.

# Contents

*Introduction*

When you have questions, God has answers!

*God's Wisdom for Your Life* is a compilation of more than a thousand Bible verses, categorized under seventy key life topics. Drawing from varied Bible translations for ease of reading, this book features subjects such as Anger, Comfort, Forgiveness, God's Love, the Holy Spirit, Patience, Peace, Prayer, Salvation, Trust, Wisdom, and Worry.

Each category is accompanied by a contemporary "life application" introduction, while quotations, prayers, and brief devotional thoughts are also scattered throughout— making *God's Wisdom for Your Life* your one-stop resource for encouragement, challenge, and hope.

■ ■ ■

# I

## Abiding

Abiding in God means we trust in Him and live with our entire lives centered on our Lord. This is more than lip-service "faith"; it means putting our money where our mouths are when we face everyday difficulties. But we can't do this under our own power. God fills us with His Spirit so we can abide in Him. When life doesn't seem to be going in the right direction, abiding can be a real challenge. But we abide either in Christ or in something else. How we're living tells us and others where our lives are focused. Where is our trust today?

"Abide in Me, and I in you. As the branch cannot bear fruit of itself, unless it abides in the vine, neither can you, unless you abide in Me. I am the vine, you are the branches. He who abides in Me, and I in him, bears much fruit; for without Me you can do nothing."
JOHN 15:4–5 NKJV

*The branch of the vine does not worry and toil and rush here to seek for sunshine and there to find rain. No; it rests in union and communion with the vine; and at the right time, and in the right way, is the right fruit found on it. Let us so abide in the Lord Jesus.*
HUDSON TAYLOR

He who dwells in the shelter of the Most High
will abide in the shadow of the Almighty.
PSALM 91:1 NASB

They that trust in the LORD shall be as mount Zion,
which cannot be removed, but abideth for ever.
PSALM 125:1 KJV

*You may trust in the Lord too little,
but you can never trust Him too much.*
ANONYMOUS

And I will pray the Father, and he shall give you another
Comforter, that he may abide with you for ever.
JOHN 14:16 KJV

*Abiding in God changes our relationship with our fellow humans.
We cannot keep our heads in the clouds as we walk with Jesus on earth.
We must deal day by day with others and through our actions
show them the love we have received.*

He that loveth his brother abideth in the light,
and there is none occasion of stumbling in him.
1 JOHN 2:10 KJV


Whosoever abideth in him sinneth not: whosoever
sinneth hath not seen him, neither known him.
1 JOHN 3:6 KJV


As the Father loved Me, I also have loved you; abide in My love.
If you keep My commandments, you will abide in My love, just as
I have kept My Father's commandments and abide in His love.
JOHN 15:9–10 NKJV


I have come as a light into the world, that whoever
believes in Me should not abide in darkness.
JOHN 12:46 NKJV


*Abiding is an active service of trust in God that demands
much of us but also provides us with untold blessings.*


If you abide in Me, and My words abide in you, you will ask what
you desire, and it shall be done for you. By this My Father is
glorified, that you bear much fruit; so you will be My disciples.
JOHN 15:7–8 NKJV


He that saith he abideth in him ought himself
also so to walk, even as he walked.
1 JOHN 2:6 KJV


*To abide with Christ—to stay with Him and to learn from Him—
is to continually receive eyes to see, ears to hear, and a heart to obey.*
ANGELA MCGUFFEY

Now he who keeps His commandments abides in Him,
and He in him. And by this we know that He abides in us,
by the Spirit whom He has given us.
1 JOHN 3:24 NKJV

Whosoever hateth his brother is a murderer: and ye
know that no murderer hath eternal life abiding in him.
1 JOHN 3:15 KJV

Whoever transgresses and does not abide in the doctrine of
Christ does not have God. He who abides in the doctrine of
Christ has both the Father and the Son.
2 JOHN 1:9 NKJV

> *Keep your life so constant in its contact with God that*
> *His surprising power may break out on the right hand and*
> *on the left. Always be in a state of expectancy, and see*
> *that you leave room for God to come in as He likes.*
> OSWALD CHAMBERS

And now, little children, abide in him; that,
when he shall appear, we may have confidence,
and not be ashamed before him at his coming.
1 JOHN 2:28 KJV

# 2
## *Abortion*

As Christians, we go against the flow of today's culture when we take a firm stand against abortion. But objecting to abortion is no mere quirk on the part of believers. Christians are called to live in a way that glorifies God, who made humanity in His own image and places a great value on each person. So highly did our heavenly Father value us that He sent His Son to die for us. Though some people may consider life cheap, God doesn't.

So God created man in his own image, in the image of
God created he him; male and female created he them.
GENESIS 1:27 KJV

*Abortion is advocated only by persons
who have themselves been born.*
RONALD REAGAN

In his hand is the life of every creature
and the breath of all mankind.
JOB 12:10 NIV

The Spirit of God has made me;
the breath of the Almighty gives me life.
JOB 33:4 NIV

You shall not murder.
EXODUS 20:13 NIV

*The greatest destroyer of peace is abortion because if a mother can kill
her own child, what is left but for me to kill you and you to kill me?
There is nothing between.*
MOTHER TERESA

If people are fighting and hit a pregnant woman and she gives
birth prematurely but there is no serious injury, the offender must
be fined whatever the woman's husband demands and the court
allows. But if there is serious injury, you are to take life for life,
eye for eye, tooth for tooth, hand for hand, foot for foot.
EXODUS 21:22–24 NIV

*The offspring of the woman, Jesus Christ, came into the world to save women who have dethroned God, taken His place, defined personhood as tissue, and willed the death of their own child. It can't be reversed, but it can be forgiven. That is why Christ died.*

JOHN PIPER

Anyone who takes the life of a human
being is to be put to death.
LEVITICUS 24:17 NIV

My frame was not hidden from you when I was made in the
secret place, when I was woven together in the depths of the
earth. Your eyes saw my unformed body; all the days ordained
for me were written in your book before one of them came to be.
PSALM 139:15–16 NIV

Before I formed you in the womb I knew you,
and before you were born I consecrated you;
I have appointed you a prophet to the nations.
JEREMIAH 1:5 NASB

*Every man's life is a plan of God.*

HORACE BUSHNELL

For he will be great in the sight of the Lord; and he
will drink no wine or liquor, and he will be filled with
the Holy Spirit while yet in his mother's womb.
LUKE 1:15 NASB

Lo, children are an heritage of the LORD: and the fruit of the
womb is his reward. As arrows are in the hand of a mighty man;
so are children of the youth. Happy is the man that hath his
quiver full of them: they shall not be ashamed, but they shall
speak with the enemies in the gate.
PSALM 127:3–5 KJV

# 3
## Addiction

Scripture does not mention many specific addictions,
like gambling or drugs, but it clearly warns against
overdrinking and sets forth principles that make it clear
that believers should not engage in an addictive lifestyle.

Do not join those who drink too much wine or gorge
themselves on meat, for drunkards and gluttons
become poor, and drowsiness clothes them in rags.
PROVERBS 23:20–21 NIV

If someone has a stubborn and rebellious son who does not
obey his father and mother and will not listen to them when they
discipline him, his father and mother shall take hold of him and
bring him to the elders at the gate of his town. They shall say to
the elders, "This son of ours is stubborn and rebellious. He will
not obey us. He is a glutton and a drunkard." Then all the men of
his town shall stone him to death. You must purge the evil from
among you. All Israel will hear of it and be afraid.
DEUTERONOMY 21:18–21 NIV

But be on your guard. Don't let the sharp edge of your
expectation get dulled by parties and drinking and shopping.
Otherwise, that Day is going to take you by complete surprise,
spring on you suddenly like a trap, for it's going to come on
everyone, everywhere, at once.
LUKE 21:34–35 MSG

> *When any small adversity befalleth us, we are too quickly dejected*
> *and turn ourselves to human comforts. If we would endeavor,*
> *like men of courage, to stand in the battle, surely we should*
> *feel the favorable assistance of God from heaven.*
> THOMAS À KEMPIS

Let us behave decently, as in the daytime, not in
carousing and drunkenness, not in sexual immorality
and debauchery, not in dissension and jealousy.
ROMANS 13:13 NIV

Jesus answered them, "Truly, truly, I say to you,
everyone who commits sin is the slave of sin."
JOHN 8:34 NASB

*Sin is a sovereign till sovereign grace dethrones it.*
C. H. SPURGEON

Therefore, dear brothers and sisters, you have no obligation to
do what your sinful nature urges you to do. For if you live by its
dictates, you will die. But if through the power of the Spirit you
put to death the deeds of your sinful nature, you will live. For all
who are led by the Spirit of God are children of God.
ROMANS 8:12–14 NLT

When you follow the desires of your sinful nature, the results are
very clear: sexual immorality, impurity, lustful pleasures, idolatry,
sorcery, hostility, quarreling, jealousy, outbursts of anger, selfish
ambition, dissension, division, envy, drunkenness, wild parties, and
other sins like these. Let me tell you again, as I have before, that
anyone living that sort of life will not inherit the Kingdom of God.
GALATIANS 5:19–21 NLT

*Drinking makes such fools of people and people are
such fools to begin with that it's compounding a felony.*
ROBERT BENCHLEY

Wine is a mocker and beer a brawler;
whoever is led astray by them is not wise.
PROVERBS 20:1 NIV

Do not let sin control the way you live;
do not give in to sinful desires.
ROMANS 6:12 NLT

The love of money causes all kinds of trouble.
Some people want money so much that they have
given up their faith and caused themselves a lot of pain.
1 TIMOTHY 6:10 CEV

*Gambling: the sure way of getting nothing for something.*
WILSON MIZNER

Don't be drunk with wine, because that will ruin your life.
Instead, be filled with the Holy Spirit.
EPHESIANS 5:18 NLT

*Of all vices, drinking is the most incompatible with greatness.*
WALTER SCOTT

I meant that you are not to associate with anyone who
claims to be a believer yet indulges in sexual sin, or is greedy,
or worships idols, or is abusive, or is a drunkard, or cheats
people. Don't even eat with such people.
1 CORINTHIANS 5:11 NLT

Don't you know that you yourselves are God's
temple and that God's Spirit dwells in your midst?
1 CORINTHIANS 3:16 NIV

If the Son gives you freedom, you are free!
JOHN 8:36 CEV

*We yearn for a free life.*
DAVID HAWKINS

# 4
## Angels

Angels are God's messengers, and they appear in numerous places in scripture. Often they carried a message from the Lord to either Israel or an individual. Mary and Joseph were visited by an angel as God prepared them for the birth of His Son. The angel of the Lord appeared at critical times in Israel's history and was sometimes a pre-incarnate appearance of Jesus. Not only do angels appear in the Old and New Testaments, scripture describes their being with Jesus at the Last Judgment. Not all angels are heavenly though. Satan and his minions fell from heaven when Satan thought to make himself greater than God. Scripture clearly describes the awful eternal destiny of these fallen angels.

And the Angel of God, who went before the camp of Israel, moved and went behind them; and the pillar of cloud went from before them and stood behind them. So it came between the camp of the Egyptians and the camp of Israel. Thus it was a cloud and darkness to the one, and it gave light by night to the other, so that the one did not come near the other all that night.
EXODUS 14:19–20 NKJV

*The angels are the dispensers and administrators of the Divine beneficence toward us; they regard our safety, undertake our defense, direct our ways, and exercise a constant solicitude that no evil befall us.*
JOHN CALVIN

The angel of the Lord found Hagar beside a spring of water in the wilderness, along the road to Shur. The angel said to her, "Hagar, Sarai's servant, where have you come from, and where are you going?" "I'm running away from my mistress, Sarai," she replied. The angel of the Lord said to her, "Return to your mistress, and submit to her authority." Then he added, "I will give you more descendants than you can count."
GENESIS 16:7–10 NLT

One day Moses was tending the flock of his father-in-law, Jethro, the priest of Midian. He led the flock far into the wilderness and came to Sinai, the mountain of God. There the angel of the LORD appeared to him in a blazing fire from the middle of a bush. Moses stared in amazement. Though the bush was engulfed in flames, it didn't burn up.
EXODUS 3:1–2 NLT

*God's restoring servants, His heavenly messengers, have encouraged, sustained, and lifted the spirits of many flagging saints; and they have changed many hopeless circumstances into bright prospects.*
BILLY GRAHAM

That night the angel of the LORD went out and put to death a hundred and eighty-five thousand in the Assyrian camp. When the people got up the next morning—there were all the dead bodies!
2 KINGS 19:35 NIV

> *For the Angel of Death spread his wings on the blast,*
> *And breathed in the face of the foe as he passed;*
> *And the eyes of the sleepers waxed deadly and chill,*
> *And their hearts but once heaved, and for ever grew still!*
> GEORGE GORDON, LORD BYRON

Then an angel of the Lord appeared to him, standing at the right side of the altar of incense. When Zechariah saw him, he was startled and was gripped with fear. But the angel said to him: "Do not be afraid, Zechariah; your prayer has been heard. Your wife Elizabeth will bear you a son, and you are to call him John. He will be a joy and delight to you, and many will rejoice because of his birth, for he will be great in the sight of the Lord. He is never to take wine or other fermented drink, and he will be filled with the Holy Spirit even before he is born. He will bring back many of the people of Israel to the Lord their God. And he will go on before the Lord, in the spirit and power of Elijah, to turn the hearts of the parents to their children and the disobedient to the wisdom of the righteous—to make ready a people prepared for the Lord."
LUKE 1:11–17 NIV

> *The angels glorify; men scrutinize: angels raise their voices in praise;*
> *men in disputation: they conceal their faces with their wings; but man*
> *with a presumptuous gaze would look into Thine unspeakable Glory.*
> JOHN CHRYSOSTOM

Now in the sixth month the angel Gabriel was sent by God to a city of Galilee named Nazareth, to a virgin betrothed to a man whose name was Joseph, of the house of David. The virgin's name was Mary. And having come in, the angel said to her, "Rejoice, highly favored one, the Lord is with you; blessed are you among women!" But when she saw him, she was troubled at his saying, and considered what manner of greeting this was. Then the angel said to her, "Do not be afraid, Mary, for you have found favor with God. And behold, you will conceive in your womb and bring forth a Son, and shall call His name JESUS."
LUKE 1:26–31 NKJV

But after he had considered this, an angel of the Lord appeared to him in a dream and said, "Joseph son of David, do not be afraid to take Mary home as your wife, because what is conceived in her is from the Holy Spirit. She will give birth to a son, and you are to give him the name Jesus, because he will save his people from their sins."
MATTHEW 1:20–21 NIV

And there were shepherds living out in the fields nearby, keeping watch over their flocks at night. An angel of the Lord appeared to them, and the glory of the Lord shone around them, and they were terrified. But the angel said to them, "Do not be afraid. I bring you good news that will cause joy for all the people. Today in the town of David a Savior has been born to you; he is the Messiah, the Lord. This will be a sign to you: You will find a baby wrapped in cloths and lying in a manger."
LUKE 2:8–12 NIV

Then he will say to those on his left, "Depart from me, you who are cursed, into the eternal fire prepared for the devil and his angels."
MATTHEW 25:41 NIV

God did not have pity on the angels that sinned.
He had them tied up and thrown into the dark
pits of hell until the time of judgment.
2 PETER 2:4 CEV

And I am convinced that nothing can ever separate us from
God's love. Neither death nor life, neither angels nor demons,
neither our fears for today nor our worries about tomorrow—
not even the powers of hell can separate us from God's love.
ROMANS 8:38 NLT

"Likewise, I say to you, there is joy in the presence of the angels
of God over one sinner who repents."
LUKE 15:10 NKJV

*Jesus' response to a frivolous question about a woman who had
married numerous brothers compared the believer's state to that of
angels and gave us a glimpse of eternity (Luke 20:27–40).*

Jesus answered and said to them, "The sons of this age
marry and are given in marriage. But those who are counted
worthy to attain that age, and the resurrection from the dead,
neither marry nor are given in marriage; nor can they die
anymore, for they are equal to the angels and are sons of God,
being sons of the resurrection."
LUKE 20:34–36 NKJV

Don't forget to show hospitality to strangers, for some who have
done this have entertained angels without realizing it!
HEBREWS 13:2 NLT

Don't you realize that we will judge angels? So you
should surely be able to resolve ordinary disputes in this life.
1 CORINTHIANS 6:3 NLT

They were told that their messages were not for themselves,
but for you. And now this Good News has been announced
to you by those who preached in the power of the Holy Spirit
sent from heaven. It is all so wonderful that even the angels are
eagerly watching these things happen.
1 PETER 1:12 NLT

When the Son of Man comes in his glory with all of his angels,
he will sit on his royal throne.
MATTHEW 25:31 CEV

# 5

## Anger

God doesn't tell us to never be angry, but He does
command us to use anger wisely. When we become angry
over wrongdoing, as He does, we may do so without
sin. But selfish, impulsive anger is almost always wrong.
Sin is the one thing that makes God angry. His is a
holy anger that punishes the wrongdoer. But anyone
who honestly seeks His forgiveness readily receives it.

You must not worship any of the gods of neighboring nations, for the LORD your God, who lives among you, is a jealous God. His anger will flare up against you, and he will wipe you from the face of the earth.

DEUTERONOMY 6:14–15 NLT

We wither beneath your anger; we are overwhelmed by your fury. You spread out our sins before you— our secret sins—and you see them all. We live our lives beneath your wrath, ending our years with a groan.

PSALM 90:7–9 NLT

*Christ took our sins and the sins of the whole world as well as the Father's wrath on His shoulders, and He has drowned them both in Himself so that we are thereby reconciled to God and become completely righteous.*

MARTIN LUTHER

For his anger lasts only a moment, but his favor lasts a lifetime! Weeping may last through the night, but joy comes with the morning.

PSALM 30:5 NLT

The Lord is compassionate and merciful, slow to get angry and filled with unfailing love.

PSALM 103:8 NLT

Then the LORD said to Cain, "Why are you angry? Why is your face downcast? If you do what is right, will you not be accepted? But if you do not do what is right, sin is crouching at your door; it desires to have you, but you must rule over it."

GENESIS 4:6–7 NIV

"Don't sin by letting anger control you." Don't let
the sun go down while you are still angry,
for anger gives a foothold to the devil.
EPHESIANS 4:26–27 NLT

> *Wise anger is like the fire from the flint; there is a great ado to*
> *bring it out; and when it does come, it is out again immediately.*
> MATTHEW HENRY

For wrath killeth the foolish man, and envy slayeth the silly one.
JOB 5:2 KJV

Better to dwell in the wilderness,
than with a contentious and angry woman.
PROVERBS 21:19 NKJV

A soft answer turns away wrath, but a harsh word stirs up anger.
PROVERBS 15:1 NKJV

> *The best remedy for a short temper is a long walk.*
> JACQUELINE SCHIFF

It's smart to be patient, but it's stupid to lose your temper.
PROVERBS 14:29 CEV

Don't make friends with anyone who has a bad temper.
PROVERBS 22:24 CEV

> *If we followed the advice in this verse (Proverbs 22:24), how*
> *many of us would have friends? Yet how true it is: if we want good*
> *relationships with others, we need to treat them well.*

An angry person stirs up conflict,
and a hot-tempered person commits many sins.
PROVERBS 29:22 NIV


Fathers, provoke not your children to anger,
lest they be discouraged.
COLOSSIANS 3:21 KJV


*The peculiarity of ill temper is that it is the vice of the virtuous.*
*It is often the one blot on an otherwise noble character.*
HENRY DRUMMOND


But I say, if you are even angry with someone, you are subject
to judgment! If you call someone an idiot, you are in danger of
being brought before the court. And if you curse someone,
you are in danger of the fires of hell.
MATTHEW 5:22 NLT


Wherefore, my beloved brethren, let every man be swift to hear,
slow to speak, slow to wrath: for the wrath of man worketh not
the righteousness of God.
JAMES 1:19–20 KJV

# 6

## Backsliding

Though God calls His people to a lifetime
commitment to Him, sin so easily distracts us
from our goal. But even as we're pulled away from
Him by the lures of Satan, God calls us to return
to Him and love Him with an undivided heart.

Those who trust in God are like Zion Mountain: nothing can move
it, a rock-solid mountain you can always depend on. Mountains
encircle Jerusalem, and God encircles his people—always has and
always will. The fist of the wicked will never violate what is due
the righteous, provoking wrongful violence. Be good to your good
people, God, to those whose hearts are right! God will round up the
backsliders, corral them with the incorrigibles. Peace over Israel!
PSALM 125:1–5 MSG


Backsliders get what they deserve;
good people receive their reward.
PROVERBS 14:14 NLT


They will never again pollute themselves with their idols
and vile images and rebellion, for I will save them from
their sinful backsliding. I will cleanse them. Then they
will truly be my people, and I will be their God.
EZEKIEL 37:23 NLT


"How boastful you are about the valleys! Your valley is flowing
away, O backsliding daughter who trusts in her treasures, saying,
'Who will come against me?' Behold, I am going to bring terror
upon you," declares the Lord God of hosts, "from all directions
around you; and each of you will be driven out headlong,
with no one to gather the fugitives together."
JEREMIAH 49:4–5 NASB


Then the LORD said to Cain, "Why are you angry? Why is your
face downcast? If you do what is right, will you not be accepted?
But if you do not do what is right, sin is crouching at your door;
it desires to have you, but you must rule over it."
GENESIS 4:6–7 NIV

Surely as a wife treacherously departeth from her husband, so have ye dealt treacherously with me, O house of Israel, saith the LORD. A voice was heard upon the high places, weeping and supplications of the children of Israel: for they have perverted their way, and they have forgotten the LORD their God. Return, ye backsliding children, and I will heal your backslidings. Behold, we come unto thee; for thou art the LORD our God.
JEREMIAH 3:20–22 KJV

*Man-like is it to fall into sin,*
*Fiend-like is it to dwell therein;*
*Christ-like is it for sin to grieve,*
*God-like is it all sin to leave.*
FRIEDRICH, FREIHERR VON LOGAU

*For every one that definitely turns his back on Christ, there*
*are hundreds who drift from Him. Life's ocean is full of currents,*
*any one of which will sweep us past the harbor-mouth even*
*when we seem nearest to it, and carry us far out to sea.*
F. B. MEYER

For, as I have often told you before and now say again even with tears, many live as enemies of the cross of Christ. Their destiny is destruction, their god is their stomach, and their glory is in their shame. Their mind is set on earthly things.
PHILIPPIANS 3:18–19 NIV

If my people, who are called by my name, will humble themselves and pray and seek my face and turn from their wicked ways, then I will hear from heaven and I will forgive their sin and will heal their land.
2 CHRONICLES 7:14 NIV

"Your own wickedness will correct you, and your backslidings will rebuke you. Know therefore and see that it is an evil and bitter thing that you have forsaken the LORD your God, and the fear of Me is not in you," says the LORD God of hosts.
JEREMIAH 2:19 NKJV

*Sin and dandelions are a whole lot alike—*
*they're a lifetime fight that you never quite win.*
WILLIAM ALLEN WHITE

Go and proclaim these words toward the north, and say: "Return, backsliding Israel," says the LORD; "I will not cause My anger to fall on you. For I am merciful," says the LORD; "I will not remain angry forever. Only acknowledge your iniquity, that you have transgressed against the LORD your God, and have scattered your charms to alien deities under every green tree, and you have not obeyed My voice," says the LORD. "Return, O backsliding children," says the LORD; "for I am married to you. I will take you, one from a city and two from a family, and I will bring you to Zion. And I will give you shepherds according to My heart, who will feed you with knowledge and understanding."
JEREMIAH 3:12–15 NKJV

O Israel, return to the LORD your God, for you have stumbled because of your iniquity; take words with you, and return to the LORD. Say to Him, "Take away all iniquity; receive us graciously, for we will offer the sacrifices of our lips. Assyria shall not save us, we will not ride on horses, nor will we say anymore to the work of our hands, 'You are our gods.' For in You the fatherless finds mercy." "I will heal their backsliding," [God declared.] "I will love them freely, for My anger has turned away from him."
HOSEA 14:1–4 NKJV

*Like Israel in Hosea's day, we have to make a choice: to depend on the enemy or the Lord. Do we look to Satan or our gracious Lord Jesus?*

Then Jesus said to his disciples, "Whoever wants to be my disciple must deny themselves and take up their cross and follow me."
MATTHEW 16:24 NIV

*Before we can begin to see the cross as something done for us, we have to see it as something done by us.*
JOHN STOTT

Fixing our eyes on Jesus, the pioneer and perfecter of faith. For the joy set before him he endured the cross, scorning its shame, and sat down at the right hand of the throne of God.
HEBREWS 12:2 NIV

# 7
## Blessings

God blesses His people when He gives them good
things and provides for them physically and spiritually.
Scripture is full of examples of people who were blessed
because they followed God. Our Lord does not want
us to hoard our blessings. Instead we need to pass
them on to others as part of our Christian lives.

The LORD had said to Abram, "Leave your native country, your relatives, and your father's family, and go to the land that I will show you. I will make you into a great nation. I will bless you and make you famous, and you will be a blessing to others. I will bless those who bless you and curse those who treat you with contempt. All the families on earth will be blessed through you."
GENESIS 12:1–3 NLT

Blessings are on the head of the righteous,
but violence covers the mouth of the wicked.
PROVERBS 10:6 NKJV

*If our only blessings were possessions, in heaven we would
be the poorest of souls. But because God made Himself
our best blessing, we are rich both here and for eternity.*

LORD, you alone are my inheritance, my cup of blessing.
You guard all that is mine.
PSALM 16:5 NLT

Then Jesus turned to his disciples and said, "God blesses you who are poor, for the Kingdom of God is yours. God blesses you who are hungry now, for you will be satisfied. God blesses you who weep now, for in due time you will laugh. What blessings await you when people hate you and exclude you and mock you and curse you as evil because you follow the Son of Man. When that happens, be happy! Yes, leap for joy! For a great reward awaits you in heaven. And remember, their ancestors treated the ancient prophets that same way.
LUKE 6:20–23 NLT

From his abundance we have all received one gracious blessing
after another. For the law was given through Moses, but God's
unfailing love and faithfulness came through Jesus Christ.
JOHN 1:16–17 NLT

*God's blessings are dispersed according to the riches*
*of His grace, not according to the depth of our faith.*
MAX LUCADO

Through Christ Jesus, God has blessed the Gentiles with the
same blessing he promised to Abraham, so that we who are
believers might receive the promised Holy Spirit through faith.
GALATIANS 3:14 NLT

The LORD bless you, and keep you; the LORD make His
face shine on you, and be gracious to you; the LORD lift
up His countenance on you, and give you peace.
NUMBERS 6:24–26 NASB

*To love God is the greatest of virtues;*
*to be loved by God is the greatest of blessings.*
PORTUGUESE PROVERB

I will bless the LORD at all times; His praise shall continually
be in my mouth. My soul will make its boast in the LORD;
the humble will hear it and rejoice.
PSALM 34:1–2 NASB

*Lord, like Israelites who entered the Promised Land,*
*we are thankful we may choose to receive Your blessings,*
*no matter how many troubles come into our lives.*

Today I have given you the choice between life and death, between blessings and curses. Now I call on heaven and earth to witness the choice you make. Oh, that you would choose life, so that you and your descendants might live! You can make this choice by loving the LORD your God, obeying him, and committing yourself firmly to him. This is the key to your life. And if you love and obey the LORD, you will live long in the land the LORD swore to give your ancestors Abraham, Isaac, and Jacob.
DEUTERONOMY 30:19–20 NLT

LORD, you are mine! I promise to obey your words! With all my heart I want your blessings. Be merciful as you promised. I pondered the direction of my life, and I turned to follow your laws.
PSALM 119:57–59 NLT

Those who live only to satisfy their own sinful nature will harvest decay and death from that sinful nature. But those who live to please the Spirit will harvest everlasting life from the Spirit. So let's not get tired of doing what is good. At just the right time we will reap a harvest of blessing if we don't give up. Therefore, whenever we have the opportunity, we should do good to everyone—especially to those in the family of faith.
GALATIANS 6:8–10 NLT

It came about that from the time he made him overseer in his house and over all that he owned, the Lord blessed the Egyptian's house on account of Joseph; thus the LORD's blessing was upon all that he owned, in the house and in the field.
GENESIS 39:5 NASB

*We are to turn our back upon evil, and in every way possible,*
*do good, help people, and bring blessings into their lives.*
NORMAN VINCENT PEALE

The godly always give generous loans to others,
and their children are a blessing.
PSALM 37:26 NLT

"Bring all the tithes into the storehouse so there will be enough
food in my Temple. If you do," says the LORD of Heaven's Armies,
"I will open the windows of heaven for you. I will pour out a
blessing so great you won't have enough room to take it in!
Try it! Put me to the test!"
MALACHI 3:10 NLT

Sing to the LORD, bless His name; proclaim good
tidings of His salvation from day to day.
PSALM 96:2 NASB

*Not only does God bless us, we bless others*
*as we share His blessings with them.*

Her children rise up and call her blessed; her husband also,
and he praises her: "Many daughters have done well,
but you excel them all."
PROVERBS 31:28–29 NKJV

But I say to you who hear, love your enemies,
do good to those who hate you, bless those who
curse you, pray for those who mistreat you.
LUKE 6:27–28 NASB

# 8

## Church

The church is both a spiritual entity and a physical
one. Because He dwells in them and works out His
plan through them, God's people are His church. Yet
those people are also gathered together in communion
and often have physical buildings. Wherever people
who love Him are gathered together, God is there.

God has put all things under the authority of Christ and
has made him head over all things for the benefit of the church.
And the church is his body; it is made full and complete by
Christ, who fills all things everywhere with himself.
EPHESIANS 1:22–23 NLT

> *The Christian does not go to the temple to worship. The Christian*
> *takes the temple with him or her. Jesus lifts us beyond the building*
> *and pays the human body the highest compliment by making*
> *it His dwelling place, the place where He meets with us.*
> RAVI ZACHARIAS

Christ also loved the church and gave Himself for her,
that He might sanctify and cleanse her with the washing
of water by the word, that He might present her to Himself
a glorious church, not having spot or wrinkle or any such
thing, but that she should be holy and without blemish.
EPHESIANS 5:25–27 NKJV

> *The uniqueness of the church is her message—the gospel.*
> *The church is the only institution entrusted by God with the message*
> *of repentance of sins and belief in Jesus Christ for forgiveness.*
> MARK DEVER AND PAUL ALEXANDER

Now these are the gifts Christ gave to the church: the apostles,
the prophets, the evangelists, and the pastors and teachers.
Their responsibility is to equip God's people to do his work
and build up the church, the body of Christ.
EPHESIANS 4:11–12 NLT

So I will call you Peter, which means "a rock." On this rock I will
build my church, and death itself will not have any power over it.
MATTHEW 16:18 CEV

We will speak the truth in love, growing in every way more and more like Christ, who is the head of his body, the church. He makes the whole body fit together perfectly. As each part does its own special work, it helps the other parts grow, so that the whole body is healthy and growing and full of love.
EPHESIANS 4:15–16 NLT

*God's children should learn to rid the church of problems,*
*not to add problems to the church.*
WATCHMAN NEE

If the follower refuses to listen to them, report the matter to the church. Anyone who refuses to listen to the church must be treated like an unbeliever or a tax collector.
MATTHEW 18:17 CEV

Those who sin should be reprimanded in front of the whole church; this will serve as a strong warning to others.
1 TIMOTHY 5:20 NLT

My friends, I beg you to watch out for anyone who causes trouble and divides the church by refusing to do what all of you were taught. Stay away from them!
ROMANS 16:17 CEV

*A church should be a powerhouse, where sluggish*
*spirits can get recharged and reanimated.*
SAMUEL A. ELIOT

But God composed the body, having given greater honor to that part which lacks it, that there should be no schism in the body, but that the members should have the same care for one another. And if one member suffers, all the members suffer with it; or if one member is honored, all the members rejoice with it. Now you are the body of Christ, and members individually.
1 CORINTHIANS 12:24–27 NKJV

# 9

## Comfort

The Holy Spirit is often called the Comforter because
He comes alongside us and helps us to live out our daily
faith. But throughout scripture, God also promises to
comfort those who suffer affliction and hardship.
We are not alone in the tough moments of our lives!

Shout for joy, you heavens; rejoice, you earth; burst into song, you mountains! For the LORD comforts his people and will have compassion on his afflicted ones.
ISAIAH 49:13 NIV

*Comfort is not the absence of problems;*
*comfort is the strength to face my problems.*
KEN HUTCHERSON

Even though I walk through the darkest valley, I will fear no evil, for you are with me; your rod and your staff, they comfort me.
PSALM 23:4 NIV

You have allowed me to suffer much hardship, but you will restore me to life again and lift me up from the depths of the earth. You will restore me to even greater honor and comfort me once again.
PSALM 71:20–21 NLT

Give me a sign of your goodness, that my enemies may see it and be put to shame, for you, LORD, have helped me and comforted me.
PSALM 86:17 NIV

Remember the word to Your servant, in which You have made me hope. This is my comfort in my affliction, that Your word has revived me.
PSALM 119:49–50 NASB

God blesses those people who grieve. They will find comfort!
MATTHEW 5:4 CEV

*If you look for truth, you may find comfort in the end;*
*if you look for comfort you will not get either comfort or truth.*
C. S. LEWIS

I find true comfort, LORD, because
your laws have stood the test of time.
PSALM 119:52 CEV

*There is a difference between receiving comfort and being comfortable.*
*God's comfort comes to those who suffer for their faith,*
*not those who are resting on their laurels.*

But woe to you who are rich, for you
have already received your comfort.
LUKE 6:24 NIV

Praise be to the God and Father of our Lord Jesus Christ, the
Father of compassion and the God of all comfort, who comforts
us in all our troubles, so that we can comfort those in any trouble
with the comfort we ourselves receive from God. For just as we
share abundantly in the sufferings of Christ, so also our comfort
abounds through Christ.
2 CORINTHIANS 1:3–5 NIV

Christ encourages you, and his love comforts you.
God's Spirit unites you, and you are concerned for others.
PHILIPPIANS 2:1 CEV

I serve you, LORD. Comfort me with your love,
just as you have promised.
PSALM 119:76 CEV

When people sin, you should forgive and comfort them,
so they won't give up in despair.
2 CORINTHIANS 2:7 CEV

> *The world hardly knows the meaning of comfort. But the Spirit of God offers the best there is to have. When we come to Him in pain and faith, He touches our hearts in tender ways that no human can. Not only does He offer a shoulder to cry on, He uses His people to strengthen and encourage hurting Christian hearts.*

God our Father loves us. He is kind and has
given us eternal comfort and a wonderful hope.
2 THESSALONIANS 2:16 CEV

# 10

## Compassion

In a rough-and-tumble world, there's great need for compassion. Hurting people seek it and often receive the hardness of this world instead. Compassion is one of Christianity's hallmarks. When we offer it to others, we reflect God's love and draw sinners to Him.

Then the LORD passed by in front of [Moses] and proclaimed, "The LORD, the LORD God, compassionate and gracious, slow to anger, and abounding in lovingkindness and truth; who keeps lovingkindness for thousands, who forgives iniquity, transgression and sin; yet He will by no means leave the guilty unpunished, visiting the iniquity of fathers on the children and on the grandchildren to the third and fourth generations."
EXODUS 34:6–7 NASB

If you seek GOD, your God, you'll be able to find him if you're serious, looking for him with your whole heart and soul. When troubles come and all these awful things happen to you, in future days you will come back to GOD, your God, and listen obediently to what he says. GOD, your God, is above all a compassionate God. In the end he will not abandon you, he won't bring you to ruin, he won't forget the covenant with your ancestors which he swore to them.
DEUTERONOMY 4:29–31 MSG

> *Man may dismiss compassion from his heart, but God never will.*
> WILLIAM COWPER

The LORD is compassionate and gracious, slow to anger and abounding in lovingkindness. He will not always strive with us, nor will He keep His anger forever.
PSALM 103:8–9 NASB

Just as a father has compassion on his children,
so the LORD has compassion on those who fear Him.
PSALM 103:13 NASB

*Jesus, Thou art all compassion,*
*Pure unbounded love Thou art;*
*Visit us with Thy salvation;*
*Enter every trembling heart.*
CHARLES WESLEY

For He will deliver the needy when he cries, the poor also, and him who has no helper. He will spare the poor and needy, and will save the souls of the needy. He will redeem their life from oppression and violence; and precious shall be their blood in His sight.
PSALM 72:12–14 NKJV

Shout for joy, you heavens; rejoice, you earth; burst into song, you mountains! For the LORD comforts his people and will have compassion on his afflicted ones.
ISAIAH 49:13 NIV

Bless the LORD, O my soul, and all that is within me, bless His holy name. Bless the LORD, O my soul, and forget none of His benefits; who pardons all your iniquities, who heals all your diseases; who redeems your life from the pit, who crowns you with lovingkindness and compassion.
PSALM 103:1–4 NASB

Remember, O LORD, Your compassion and Your lovingkindnesses, For they have been from of old.
PSALM 25:6 NASB

You, O LORD, will not withhold Your compassion from me;
Your lovingkindness and Your truth will continually preserve me.
PSALM 40:11 NASB

Have mercy on me, O God, according to your unfailing love;
according to your great compassion blot out my transgressions.
PSALM 51:1 NIV

May the flood of water not overflow me nor the deep swallow
me up, nor the pit shut its mouth on me. Answer me, O LORD,
for Your lovingkindness is good; according to the greatness of
Your compassion, turn to me.
PSALM 69:15–16 NASB

[Mankind's] heart was not steadfast toward Him, nor were they
faithful in His covenant. But He, being compassionate, forgave
their iniquity and did not destroy them; and often He restrained
His anger and did not arouse all His wrath. Thus He remembered
that they were but flesh, a wind that passes and does not return.
PSALM 78:37–39 NASB

He who conceals his transgressions will not prosper, but he
who confesses and forsakes them will find compassion.
PROVERBS 28:13 NASB

> *Biblical orthodoxy without compassion is*
> *surely the ugliest thing in the world.*
> FRANCIS SCHAEFFER

Light shines in the darkness for the godly. They are generous,
compassionate, and righteous.
PSALM 112:4 NLT

So the LORD must wait for you to come to him so he can
show you his love and compassion. For the LORD is a faithful
God. Blessed are those who wait for his help.
ISAIAH 30:18 NLT

For no one is abandoned by the Lord forever. Though he
brings grief, he also shows compassion because of the
greatness of his unfailing love. For he does not enjoy
hurting people or causing them sorrow.
LAMENTATIONS 3:31–33 NLT

*If we want to touch hearts for Christ, the gentle, tender virtue of
compassion could mean more than a thousand words of argument.*

You must be compassionate,
just as your Father is compassionate.
LUKE 6:36 NLT

*Christianity demands a level of caring
that transcends human inclinations.*
ERWIN W. LUTZER

Are your hearts tender and compassionate? Then make me truly
happy by agreeing wholeheartedly with each other, loving one
another, and working together with one mind and purpose.
PHILIPPIANS 2:1–2 NLT

*The measure of a country's greatness is its
ability to retain compassion in times of crisis.*
THURGOOD MARSHALL

If someone has enough money to live well and sees
a brother or sister in need but shows no compassion—
how can God's love be in that person?
1 JOHN 3:17 NLT

# II

## Conservation

Though God does not explain how to solve all
of our conservation problems, He tells us about
His creation of the earth and the stewardship
role He expects humans to fulfill.

In the beginning God created the heaven and the earth.
GENESIS 1:1 KJV

And God said, Let us make man in our image, after our likeness:
and let them have dominion over the fish of the sea, and over
the fowl of the air, and over the cattle, and over all the earth, and
over every creeping thing that creepeth upon the earth.
GENESIS 1:26 KJV

> *God has given us the earth to have dominion over it.*
> *We must remember that this is the only place*
> *we have to live in and treat it accordingly.*

And God blessed them, and God said unto them, Be fruitful,
and multiply, and replenish the earth, and subdue it: and have
dominion over the fish of the sea, and over the fowl of the air,
and over every living thing that moveth upon the earth.
GENESIS 1:28 KJV

> *Conservation is a state of harmony between men and land.*
> ALDO LEOPOLD

The land produced vegetation: plants bearing seed according
to their kinds and trees bearing fruit with seed in it according to
their kinds. And God saw that it was good.
GENESIS 1:12 NIV

Good people are kind to their animals,
but a mean person is cruel.
PROVERBS 12:10 CEV

The Scriptures say, "The earth and
everything in it belong to the Lord."
1 CORINTHIANS 10:26 CEV

*Each particle of matter is an immensity; each leaf a world;*
*each insect an inexplicable compendium.*

JOHANN KASPAR LAVATER

For the land which you go to possess is not like the land of
Egypt from which you have come, where you sowed your seed
and watered it by foot, as a vegetable garden; but the land which
you cross over to possess is a land of hills and valleys, which
drinks water from the rain of heaven, a land for which the LORD
your God cares; the eyes of the LORD your God are always on it,
from the beginning of the year to the very end of the year.

DEUTERONOMY 11:10–12 NKJV

# 12
## Criticism

None of us like to hear about the ways in which we haven't been perfect. But if we're honest, we'll also admit we do miss God's mark of perfection. That's why we need to listen carefully to godly critics, weighing their advice and discerning the good things they have to say. Not every criticism is accurate, but if we're wise, we'll learn from those that are.

Do everything without complaining and arguing, so that
no one can criticize you. Live clean, innocent lives as
children of God, shining like bright lights in a world full
of crooked and perverse people.
PHILIPPIANS 2:14–15 NLT

Don't speak evil against each other, dear brothers and sisters.
If you criticize and judge each other, then you are criticizing
and judging God's law. But your job is to obey the law,
not to judge whether it applies to you.
JAMES 4:11 NLT

The fear of the LORD is the beginning of wisdom:
and the knowledge of the holy is understanding.
PROVERBS 9:10 KJV

*Even the greatest of the prophets, Moses, endured criticism
from his siblings, and God stood up for him. He can
stand up for us, too, when we are serving Him.*

I, the LORD, speak to prophets in visions and dreams. But my
servant Moses is the leader of my people. He sees me face to
face, and everything I say to him is perfectly clear. You have no
right to criticize my servant Moses.
NUMBERS 12:6–8 CEV

*You've heard the expression "Job's comforters."
Who received more criticism than Job? Yet this faithful man
stood against his critics, calling them to have compassion.*

I could say the same things if you were in my place. I could spout
off criticism and shake my head at you. But if it were me, I would
encourage you. I would try to take away your grief.
JOB 16:4–5 NLT

Why do you criticize other followers of the Lord?
Why do you look down on them? The day is coming
when God will judge all of us.
ROMANS 14:10 CEV

> *People are eternally divided into two classes: the believer, builder,*
> *and praiser, and the unbeliever, destroyer, and critic.*
> JOHN RUSKIN

Now accept the one who is weak in faith, but not for the purpose
of passing judgment on his opinions. One person has faith
that he may eat all things, but he who is weak eats vegetables
only. The one who eats is not to regard with contempt the one
who does not eat, and the one who does not eat is not to judge
the one who eats, for God has accepted him. Who are you to
judge the servant of another? To his own master he stands or
falls; and he will stand, for the Lord is able to make him stand.
ROMANS 14:1–4 NASB

Use clean language that no one can criticize. Do this, and your
enemies will be too ashamed to say anything against you.
TITUS 2:8 CEV

If you listen to constructive criticism,
you will be at home among the wise.
PROVERBS 15:31 NLT

Timely advice is lovely, like golden apples in a silver basket. To one who listens, valid criticism is like a gold earring or other gold jewelry.
PROVERBS 25:11–12 NLT

In the end, people appreciate honest
criticism far more than flattery.
PROVERBS 28:23 NLT

Whoever stubbornly refuses to accept criticism
will suddenly be destroyed beyond recovery.
PROVERBS 29:1 NLT

> *Honest criticism is hard to take, particularly from*
> *a relative, a friend, an acquaintance, or a stranger.*
> FRANKLIN P. JONES

Better to be criticized by a wise person
than to be praised by a fool.
ECCLESIASTES 7:5 NLT

# 13
## Dating

Of course there was nothing like dating in the
biblical era. Marriages were generally arranged, and
couples often had little contact beforehand. But
God's standard of sexual purity is unmistakable
in both the Old and New Testaments.

Marriage should be honored by all, and the marriage bed kept
pure, for God will judge the adulterer and all the sexually immoral.
HEBREWS 13:4 NIV

If a man seduces a virgin who is not pledged to
be married and sleeps with her, he must pay the
bride-price, and she shall be his wife.
EXODUS 22:16 NIV

Blessed are the pure in heart, for they will see God.
MATTHEW 5:8 NIV

How can a young person stay pure? By obeying your word.
PSALM 119:9 NLT

Do not be unequally yoked together with unbelievers.
For what fellowship has righteousness with lawlessness?
And what communion has light with darkness?
2 CORINTHIANS 6:14 NKJV

> *By anchoring yourself with the qualities of wisdom, optimism,*
> *discernment, spirituality, joyfulness, gratitude, and empathy,*
> *you are sure to avoid some of the dizzying motion of dating.*
> *And you are far more likely to find true love.*
> LES PARROTT III

Wisdom will protect you from the smooth talk of a
sinful woman, who breaks her wedding vows and
leaves the man she married when she was young.
PROVERBS 2:16–17 CEV

*The Law's punishment for sexual moral failure
seems very harsh to us today, but it shows us how
seriously God takes premarital unfaithfulness.*

Suppose a man marries a woman, but after sleeping with her, he turns against her and publicly accuses her of shameful conduct, saying, "When I married this woman, I discovered she was not a virgin.". . . Suppose the man's accusations are true, and he can show that she was not a virgin. The woman must be taken to the door of her father's home, and there the men of the town must stone her to death, for she has committed a disgraceful crime in Israel by being promiscuous while living in her parents' home. In this way, you will purge this evil from among you.
DEUTERONOMY 22:13–14, 20–21 NLT

Treat older women as you would your mother, and treat younger women with all purity as you would your own sisters.
1 TIMOTHY 5:2 NLT

*If marriage were a career, dating would be the internship.*
GARY CHAPMAN

And now, dear brothers and sisters, one final thing. Fix your thoughts on what is true, and honorable, and right, and pure, and lovely, and admirable. Think about things that are excellent and worthy of praise.
PHILIPPIANS 4:8 NLT

*God would not rub so hard if it were not to fetch out the dirt
that is ingrained in our natures. God loves purity so well
He had rather see a hole than a spot in His child's garments.*
WILLIAM GURNALL

Run from anything that stimulates youthful lusts. Instead,
pursue righteous living, faithfulness, love, and peace. Enjoy the
companionship of those who call on the Lord with pure hearts.
2 TIMOTHY 2:22 NLT

But I say to you that whoever looks at a woman to lust for her
has already committed adultery with her in his heart.
MATTHEW 5:28 NKJV

> *The good devout man first makes inner preparation for the*
> *actions he has later to perform. His outward actions do*
> *not draw him into lust and vice; rather it is he who*
> *bends them into the shape of reason and right judgment.*
> THOMAS À KEMPIS

The acts of the flesh are obvious:
sexual immorality, impurity and debauchery.
GALATIANS 5:19 NIV

My son, obey your father's commands, and don't neglect your
mother's instruction. . . . When you walk, their counsel will lead
you. . . . For their command is a lamp and their instruction a light;
their corrective discipline is the way to life. It will keep you from
the immoral woman, from the smooth tongue of a promiscuous
woman. Don't lust for her beauty. Don't let her coy glances seduce
you. For a prostitute will bring you to poverty, but sleeping with
another man's wife will cost you your life. Can a man scoop a
flame into his lap and not have his clothes catch on fire?
PROVERBS 6:20, 22–27 NLT

# 14
## Death

In the Bible, death refers to both a physical and spiritual demise, for unrepented sin kills souls as surely as it destroys bodies. God delivers those who believe in Him from both physical and spiritual destruction.

See, I set before you today life and prosperity, death and destruction. For I command you today to love the LORD your God, to walk in obedience to him, and to keep his commands, decrees and laws; then you will live and increase, and the LORD your God will bless you in the land you are entering to possess.

DEUTERONOMY 30:15–16 NIV

Our God is a God who saves!
The Sovereign Lord rescues us from death.

PSALM 68:20 NLT

> *Death to a good man is his release from the imprisonment of this world, and his departure to the enjoyments of another world.*
>
> MATTHEW HENRY

The LORD brings death and makes alive;
he brings down to the grave and raises up.

1 SAMUEL 2:6 NIV

"I called to the LORD, who is worthy of praise, and have been saved from my enemies. The waves of death swirled about me; the torrents of destruction overwhelmed me. The cords of the grave coiled around me; the snares of death confronted me. In my distress I called to the LORD; I called out to my God. From his temple he heard my voice; my cry came to his ears."

2 SAMUEL 22:4–7 NIV

Yea, though I walk through the valley of the shadow of death, I will fear no evil: for thou art with me; thy rod and thy staff they comfort me.

PSALM 23:4 KJV

*They that love beyond the world cannot be separated by it.*
*Death cannot kill what never dies.*
WILLIAM PENN

So when this corruptible shall have put on incorruption, and this mortal shall have put on immortality, then shall be brought to pass the saying that is written, Death is swallowed up in victory. O death, where is thy sting? O grave, where is thy victory? The sting of death is sin; and the strength of sin is the law.
1 CORINTHIANS 15:54–56 KJV

He will swallow up death in victory; and the Lord GOD will wipe away tears from off all faces; and the rebuke of his people shall he take away from off all the earth: for the LORD hath spoken it.
ISAIAH 25:8 KJV

*I thank my God for graciously granting me the*
*opportunity. . .of learning that death is the key*
*which unlocks the door to our true happiness.*
WOLFGANG AMADEUS MOZART

Precious in the sight of the LORD is
the death of his faithful servants.
PSALM 116:15 NIV

Riches do not profit in the day of wrath,
but righteousness delivers from death.
PROVERBS 11:4 NKJV

*Let them fear death who do not fear sin.*
THOMAS J. WATSON SR.

When calamity comes, the wicked are brought down,
but even in death the righteous seek refuge in God.
PROVERBS 14:32 NIV

Therefore, just as sin came into the world through one man,
and death through sin, and so death spread to all men because
all sinned—for sin indeed was in the world before the law was
given, but sin is not counted where there is no law. Yet death
reigned from Adam to Moses, even over those whose sinning
was not like the transgression of Adam, who was a type of the
one who was to come.
ROMANS 5:12–14 ESV

But where sin increased, grace increased all the more, so that,
just as sin reigned in death, so also grace might reign through
righteousness to bring eternal life through Jesus Christ our Lord.
ROMANS 5:20–21 NIV

*Eternity is not something that begins after you are dead.*
*It is going on all the time. We are in it now.*
CHARLOTTE PERKINS GILMAN

Don't you know that all who share in Christ Jesus by being
baptized also share in his death? When we were baptized,
we died and were buried with Christ. We were baptized,
so that we would live a new life, as Christ was raised to
life by the glory of God the Father.
ROMANS 6:3–4 CEV

For to me, to live is Christ, and to die is gain.
PHILIPPIANS 1:21 NKJV

We know that death no longer has any power over Christ. He died and was raised to life, never again to die. When Christ died, he died for sin once and for all. But now he is alive, and he lives only for God. In the same way, you must think of yourselves as dead to the power of sin. But Christ Jesus has given life to you, and you live for God.
ROMANS 6:9–11 CEV

For the wages of sin is death, but the gift of God is eternal life in Christ Jesus our Lord.
ROMANS 6:23 NIV

*There is no better armor against the shafts of death than to be busied in God's service.*
THOMAS FULLER

The mind governed by flesh is death, but the mind governed by the Spirit is life and peace. The mind governed by the flesh is hostile to God; it does not submit to God's law, nor can it do so. Those who are in the realm of the flesh cannot please God.
ROMANS 8:6–8 NIV

Do not be afraid of those who kill the body but cannot kill the soul. Rather, be afraid of the One who can destroy both soul and body in hell.
MATTHEW 10:28 NIV

*Until our master summons us, not a hair on our head can perish, not a moment of our life be snatched from us. When He sends for us, it should seem but the message that the child is wanted at home.*
ANTHONY THOROLD

For I am persuaded that neither death nor life, nor angels nor principalities nor powers, nor things present nor things to come, nor height nor depth, nor any other created thing, shall be able to separate us from the love of God which is in Christ Jesus our Lord.
ROMANS 8:38–39 NKJV

But Christ has indeed been raised from the dead, the firstfruits of those who have fallen asleep. For since death came through a man, the resurrection of the dead comes also through a man. For as in Adam all die, so in Christ all will be made alive.
1 CORINTHIANS 15:20–22 NIV

For the sorrow that is according to the will of God produces a repentance without regret, leading to salvation, but the sorrow of the world produces death.
2 CORINTHIANS 7:10 NASB

Do not be surprised, my brothers and sisters, if the world hates you. We know that we have passed from death to life, because we love each other. Anyone who does not love remains in death. Anyone who hates a brother or sister is a murderer, and you know that no murderer has eternal life residing in him.
1 JOHN 3:13–15 NIV

*There is one single fact which we may oppose to all the wit and argument of infidelity, namely, that no man ever repented of being a Christian on his death bed.*
HANNAH MOORE

# 15
## Decision Making

When it comes to decision making, we need to
ask ourselves, Who do I get advice from? If our
primary counselor is not God, we may be headed
for trouble. But He also puts wise people in our
paths. Are we making the most of their advice?

I bless the LORD who gives me counsel; in the night also
my heart instructs me. I have set the LORD always before me;
because he is at my right hand, I shall not be shaken.
PSALM 16:7–8 ESV

> *In the darkest of nights cling to the assurance that God loves you,*
> *that He always has advice for you, a path that you can tread and a*
> *solution to your problem—and you will experience that which you*
> *believe. God never disappoints anyone who places his trust in Him.*
> BASILEA SCHLINK

You guide me with your counsel,
and afterward you will take me into glory.
PSALM 73:24 NIV

"I, wisdom, dwell with prudence, and I find knowledge and
discretion. The fear of the LORD is hatred of evil. Pride and
arrogance and the way of evil and perverted speech I hate. I
have counsel and sound wisdom; I have insight; I have strength.
By me kings reign, and rulers decree what is just."
PROVERBS 8:12–15 ESV

Today I am giving you a choice. You can choose life and success
or death and disaster. I am commanding you to be loyal to the
LORD, to live the way he has told you, and to obey his laws and
teachings. You are about to cross the Jordan River and take the
land that he is giving you. If you obey him, you will live and
become successful and powerful. On the other hand, you might
choose to disobey the LORD and reject him. So I'm warning you
that if you bow down and worship other gods, you won't have
long to live.
DEUTERONOMY 30:15–18 CEV

But if you refuse to serve the LORD, then choose today whom you will serve. Would you prefer the gods your ancestors served beyond the Euphrates? Or will it be the gods of the Amorites in whose land you now live? But as for me and my family, we will serve the LORD.
JOSHUA 24:15 NLT

Powerful LORD God, all who stay far from you will be lost, and you will destroy those who are unfaithful. It is good for me to be near you. I choose you as my protector, and I will tell about your wonderful deeds.
PSALM 73:27–28 CEV

*If knowing answers to life's questions is absolutely necessary to you, then forget the journey. You will never make it, for this is a journey of unknowables.*
JEANNE GUYON

"When your terror comes like a storm, and your destruction comes like a whirlwind, when distress and anguish come upon you. Then they will call on me, but I will not answer; they will seek me diligently, but they will not find me. Because they hated knowledge and did not choose the fear of the LORD, they would have none of my counsel and despised my every rebuke."
PROVERBS 1:27–30 NKJV

Do not envy the oppressor, and choose none of his ways; for the perverse person is an abomination to the LORD, but His secret counsel is with the upright. The curse of the LORD is on the house of the wicked, but He blesses the home of the just.
PROVERBS 3:31–33 NKJV

Blessed is the one who does not walk in step with
the wicked or stand in the way that sinners take or
sit in the company of mockers.
PSALM 1:1 NIV

A good name is rather to be chosen than great riches, and loving
favor rather than silver and gold.
PROVERBS 22:1 KJV

The thoughts of the righteous are just;
the counsels of the wicked are deceitful.
PROVERBS 12:5 ESV

*Christ told His disciples not to be anxious about tomorrow, but
He never said not to consider tomorrow. Intelligent problem solving
demands careful consideration of the future effects of present solutions.*
R. C. SPROUL

Listen to advice and accept instruction, that you may gain
wisdom in the future. Many are the plans in the mind of a
man, but it is the purpose of the LORD that will stand.
PROVERBS 19:20–21 ESV

Where there is no guidance, a people falls,
but in an abundance of counselors there is safety.
PROVERBS 11:14 ESV

Fools think they know what is best,
but a sensible person listens to advice.
PROVERBS 12:15 CEV

Without good advice everything goes wrong—
it takes careful planning for things to go right.
PROVERBS 15:22 CEV

I choose as my friends everyone who worships
you and follows your teachings.
PSALM 119:63 CEV

> *When the honest, sincere Christian is faced with the decision*
> *regarding whether a thing is right or wrong, he should ask,*
> *Does it agree with all that the scripture has to say on the subject?*
> CURTIS HUTSON

Choose good instead of evil! See that justice is done.
AMOS 5:15 CEV

# 16

## Desires

Both good and sinful desires affect us in our spiritual
walks. But God clearly tells us that He wants to give
us whatever we desire, if it aligns with His will.

The eyes of all look expectantly to You, and You give
them their food in due season. You open Your hand
and satisfy the desire of every living thing.
PSALM 145:15–17 NKJV

Take delight in the LORD, and he will
give you the desires of your heart.
PSALM 37:4 NIV

> *Give me one hundred preachers who fear nothing but sin,*
> *and desire nothing but God, and I care not a straw whether*
> *they be clergymen or laymen; such alone will shake the gates*
> *of hell and set up the kingdom of heaven on earth.*
> JOHN WESLEY

Whom have I in heaven but you? I desire you more than anything
on earth. My health may fail, and my spirit may grow weak,
but God remains the strength of my heart; he is mine forever.
PSALM 73:25–26 NLT

> *Longing desire prayeth always, though the tongue be silent.*
> *If thou art ever longing, thou art ever praying.*
> SAINT AUGUSTINE

As the deer pants for the water brooks,
so pants my soul for You, O God.
PSALM 42:1 NKJV

He grants the desires of those who fear him;
he hears their cries for help and rescues them.
PSALM 145:19 NLT

*No man should desire to be happy who is not at the same time holy.*
*He should spend his efforts in seeking to know and do the will of God,*
*leaving to Christ the matter of how happy he should be.*

A. W. TOZER

O LORD, You have heard the desire of the humble;
You will strengthen their heart, You will incline Your
ear to vindicate the orphan and the oppressed,
so that man who is of the earth will no longer cause terror.
PSALM 10:17–18 NASB

Do not envy the wicked, do not desire their company.
PROVERBS 24:1 NIV

Whoever of you loves life and desires to see many good days,
keep your tongue from evil and your lips from telling lies.
PSALM 34:12–13 NIV

*No sinful desire prospers for long. Though faithful Christians may*
*have to wait for blessings, they will surely come from God's hand.*

You shall not covet your neighbor's wife. You shall not
set your desire on your neighbor's house or land,
his male or female servant, his ox or donkey,
or anything that belongs to your neighbor.
DEUTERONOMY 5:21 NIV

Those who want to get rich fall into temptation and
a trap and into many foolish and harmful desires
that plunge people into ruin and destruction.
1 TIMOTHY 6:9 NIV

What the wicked dread will overtake them;
what the righteous desire will be granted.
PROVERBS 10:24 NIV


The desire of the righteous ends only in good;
the expectation of the wicked in wrath.
PROVERBS 11:23 ESV


How blessed is the man who finds wisdom and the man who
gains understanding. For her profit is better than the profit of
silver and her gain better than fine gold. She is more precious
than jewels; and nothing you desire compares with her.
PROVERBS 3:13–15 NASB


> *The desire of love, Joy:*
> *The desire of life, Peace:*
> *The desire of the soul, Heaven.*
> WILLIAM SHARP


And I know that nothing good lives in me, that is,
in my sinful nature. I want to do what is right, but I can't.
ROMANS 7:18 NLT


Now those who belong to Christ Jesus have
crucified the flesh with its passions and desires.
GALATIANS 5:24 NASB


Those who live according to the flesh have their minds set
on what the flesh desires; but those who live in accordance
with the Spirit have their minds set on what the Spirit desires.
ROMANS 8:5 NIV

Let love be your highest goal! But you should also desire the
special abilities the Spirit gives—
especially the ability to prophesy.
1 CORINTHIANS 14:1 NLT

*Lord, give me the desire to follow You so closely I can feel
the brush of Your robe. May living near You keep sin at bay.*

I say, walk by the Spirit, and you will
not gratify the desires of the flesh.
GALATIANS 5:16 NIV

# 17
## Discrimination

In no way does discrimination against another person fit with the Christian lifestyle. God's Word calls us to love others no matter what their nationality, skin color, or anything else. Christians should be known by their love for their fellow Christians as well as those who need to accept Christ.

"A new commandment I give to you, that you love one another; as I have loved you, that you also love one another. By this all will know that you are My disciples, if you have love for one another."
JOHN 13:34–35 NKJV

But I say to you, love your enemies, bless those who curse you, do good to those who hate you, and pray for those who spitefully use you and persecute you.
MATTHEW 5:44 NKJV

*Just as prejudice blinds unbelievers to the only way of eternal life, it blinds believers to the preciousness of every soul.*
A. CHARLES KREGAL

Love your neighbor as yourself.
MATTHEW 19:19 NLT

Peter told them, "You know it is against our laws for a Jewish man to enter a Gentile home like this or to associate with you. But God has shown me that I should no longer think of anyone as impure or unclean."
ACTS 10:28 NLT

*There is no prejudice so strong as that which arises from a fancied exemption from all prejudice.*
WILLIAM HAZLITT

We are made right with God by placing our faith in Jesus Christ. And this is true for everyone who believes, no matter who we are.
ROMANS 3:22 NLT

Just as our bodies have many parts and each part has a special function, so it is with Christ's body. We are many parts of one body, and we all belong to each other.
ROMANS 12:4–5 NLT

*If we were to wake up some morning and find*
*that everyone was the same race, creed, and color,*
*we would find some other causes for prejudice by noon.*
GEORGE AIKEN

There is neither Jew nor Gentile, neither slave nor free, nor is there male and female, for you are all one in Christ Jesus.
GALATIANS 3:28 NIV

Here there is no Gentile or Jew, circumcised or uncircumcised, barbarian, Scythian, slave or free, but Christ is all, and is in all.
COLOSSIANS 3:11 NIV

# 18

## *Divorce*

Could God's Word make it clearer what He thinks about divorce? But humans are fallen beings, and our failures often seriously impact our marriages. Our Lord's compassion and forgiveness work in our lives no matter what our married state; but that does not change the fact that He designed marriage to be a wonderful thing, joining two people for life.

The Pharisees also came to Him, testing Him, and saying to Him, "Is it lawful for a man to divorce his wife for just any reason?" And He answered and said to them, "Have you not read that He who made them at the beginning 'made them male and female,' and said, 'For this reason a man shall leave his father and mother and be joined to his wife, and the two shall become one flesh'? So then, they are no longer two but one flesh. Therefore what God has joined together, let not man separate." They said to Him, "Why then did Moses command to give a certificate of divorce, and to put her away?" He said to them, "Moses, because of the hardness of your hearts, permitted you to divorce your wives, but from the beginning it was not so. And I say to you, whoever divorces his wife, except for sexual immorality, and marries another, commits adultery; and whoever marries her who is divorced commits adultery."

MATTHEW 19:3–9 NKJV

It has been said, "Anyone who divorces his wife must give her a certificate of divorce." But I tell you that anyone who divorces his wife, except for sexual immorality, makes her the victim of adultery, and anyone who marries a divorced woman commits adultery.

MATTHEW 5:31–32 NIV

But for those who are married, I have a command that comes not from me, but from the Lord. A wife must not leave her husband. But if she does leave him, let her remain single or else be reconciled to him. And the husband must not leave his wife.

1 CORINTHIANS 7:10–11 NLT

*According to the law, adultery is the only sufficient reason for divorce.*
A. W. PINK

When a man takes a wife and marries her, and it happens that she finds no favor in his eyes because he has found some indecency in her, and he writes her a certificate of divorce and puts it in her hand and sends her out from his house, and she leaves his house and goes and becomes another man's wife, and if the latter husband turns against her and writes her a certificate of divorce and puts it in her hand and sends her out of his house, or if the latter husband dies who took her to be his wife, then her former husband who sent her away is not allowed to take her again to be his wife, since she has been defiled; for that is an abomination before the Lord, and you shall not bring sin on the land which the Lord your God gives you as an inheritance.
DEUTERONOMY 24:1–4 NASB

Another thing you do: You flood the Lord's altar with tears. You weep and wail because he no longer looks with favor on your offerings or accepts them with pleasure from your hands. You ask, "Why?" It is because the Lord is the witness between you and the wife of your youth. You have been unfaithful to her, though she is your partner, the wife of your marriage covenant. Has not the one God made you? You belong to him in body and spirit. And what does the one God seek? Godly offspring. So be on your guard, and do not be unfaithful to the wife of your youth . . . . So be on your guard, and do not be unfaithful.
MALACHI 2:13–16 NIV

And a woman who has a husband who does not believe, if he is willing to live with her, let her not divorce him. For the unbelieving husband is sanctified by the wife, and the unbelieving wife is sanctified by the husband; otherwise your children would be unclean, but now they are holy.
1 CORINTHIANS 7:13–14 NKJV

A wife should stay married to her husband until he dies. Then she is free to marry again, but only to a man who is a follower of the Lord.
1 CORINTHIANS 7:39 CEV

*Adultery is character assassination; it is the breaking of one's solemn promise; it is the treacherous betrayal of one's closest friend. Divorce involves the same kind of betrayal; it may be legal, but it is still nasty.*
DR. DAVID CRABTREE

Let your fountain be blessed, and rejoice in the wife of your youth. As a loving hind and a graceful doe, let her breasts satisfy you at all times; be exhilarated always with her love.
PROVERBS 5:18–19 NASB

Suppose a woman isn't engaged to be married, and a man talks her into sleeping with him. If they are caught, they will be forced to get married. He must give her father fifty pieces of silver as a bride-price and can never divorce her.
DEUTERONOMY 22:28–29 CEV

*In all my thirteen years as a professional marriage counselor, I've never seen an unbiblical divorce cause less pain and suffering than it would have taken to "fix" the marriage.*
LOU PRIOLO

# 19

## Doubt

Doubt comes to us easily, and we fear the trials
that bring it on. But those trials are part of our
Christian growth as we learn to trust in our Lord.

Truly I tell you, if anyone says to this mountain, "Go, throw yourself into the sea," and does not doubt in their heart but believes that what they say will happen, it will be done for them.
MARK 11:23 NIV

If any of you lacks wisdom, he should ask God, who gives generously to all without finding fault, and it will be given to you. But when you ask, you must believe and not doubt, because the one who doubts is like a wave of the sea, blown and tossed by the wind. That person should not expect to receive anything from the Lord. Such a person is double-minded and unstable in all they do.
JAMES 1:5–8 NIV

You must show mercy to those whose faith is wavering.
JUDE 1:22 NLT

But Abraham never doubted or questioned God's promise. His faith made him strong, and he gave all the credit to God.
ROMANS 4:20 CEV

My friends, watch out! Don't let evil thoughts or doubts make any of you turn from the living God.
HEBREWS 3:12 CEV

> *Worry affects the circulation, the heart, the glands,*
> *the whole nervous system. I have never known a man*
> *who died from overwork, but many who died from doubt.*
> CHARLES H. MAYO

I will therefore that men pray every where, lifting up holy hands, without wrath and doubting.
1 TIMOTHY 2:8 KIV

Yea, though I walk through the valley of the shadow
of death, I will fear no evil: for thou art with me;
thy rod and thy staff they comfort me.
PSALM 23:4 KJV

> *Light up. . .the lamp of faith in your heart. It will lead you*
> *safely through the mists of doubt and the black darkness of despair;*
> *along the narrow, thorny ways of sickness and sorrow, and over*
> *the treacherous places of temptation and uncertainty.*
> JAMES ALLEN

When doubts filled my mind, your comfort
gave me renewed hope and cheer.
PSALM 94:19 NLT

But if you have doubts about whether or not you should
eat something, you are sinning if you go ahead and do it.
For you are not following your convictions. If you do
anything you believe is not right, you are sinning.
ROMANS 14:23 NLT

# 20
# *Eternal Life*

Though God does not tell us all the details about eternity, He provides us with the road map to get there. Eternal life is available only to those who trust in His Son. Though we have earned death through sin, in Jesus we are brought to new, eternal life.

Anyone who believes in God's Son has eternal life. Anyone who
doesn't obey the Son will never experience eternal life
but remains under God's angry judgment.
JOHN 3:36 NLT

*Eternity to the godly is a day that has no sunset;*
*eternity to the wicked is a night that has no sunrise.*
THOMAS WATSON

"Very truly I tell you, whoever hears my word and believes him
who sent me has eternal life and will not be judged
but has crossed over from death to life."
JOHN 5:24 NIV

"My sheep hear My voice, and I know them, and they follow Me.
And I give them eternal life, and they shall never perish;
neither shall anyone snatch them out of My hand. My Father,
who has given them to Me, is greater than all; and no one
is able to snatch them out of My Father's hand."
JOHN 10:27–29 NKJV

Someone came to Jesus with this question: "Teacher, what
good deed must I do to have eternal life?" "Why ask me about
what is good?" Jesus replied. "There is only One who is good.
But to answer your question—if you want to receive eternal life,
keep the commandments."
MATTHEW 19:16–17 NLT

Everyone who has left houses or brothers or sisters or father
or mother or wife or children or lands, for My name's sake,
shall receive a hundredfold, and inherit eternal life.
MATTHEW 19:29 NKJV

"What sorrow awaits the world, because it tempts people to sin. Temptations are inevitable, but what sorrow awaits the person who does the tempting. So if your hand or foot causes you to sin, cut it off and throw it away. It's better to enter eternal life with only one hand or one foot than to be thrown into eternal fire with both of your hands and feet. And if your eye causes you to sin, gouge it out and throw it away. It's better to enter eternal life with only one eye than to have two eyes and be thrown into the fire of hell."

MATTHEW 18:7–9 NLT

*Nothing can separate you from God's love, absolutely nothing. God is enough for time, God is enough for eternity. God is enough!*

HANNAH WHITALL SMITH

"For God loved the world so much that he gave his one and only Son, so that everyone who believes in him will not perish but have eternal life."

JOHN 3:16 NLT

*The best we can hope for in this life is a knothole peek at the shining realities ahead. Yet a glimpse is enough. It's enough to convince our hearts that whatever sufferings and sorrows currently assail us aren't worthy of comparison to that which waits over the horizon.*

JONI EARECKSON TADA

God will reward each of us for what we have done. He will give eternal life to everyone who has patiently done what is good in the hope of receiving glory, honor, and life that lasts forever. But he will show how angry and furious he can be with every selfish person who rejects the truth and wants to do evil.

ROMANS 2:6–8 CEV

So just as sin ruled over all people and brought them to death, now God's wonderful grace rules instead, giving us right standing with God and resulting in eternal life through Jesus Christ our Lord.
ROMANS 5:21 NLT

For the wages of sin is death, but the gift of God is eternal life in Christ Jesus our Lord.
ROMANS 6:23 NKJV

*Lord, Your Word has given me a vision of eternity,*
*and the Spirit speaks of its certainty in my heart.*
*Let those who doubt never turn me from it.*

For you have been born again, but not to a life that will quickly end. Your new life will last forever because it comes from the eternal, living word of God.
1 PETER 1:23 NLT

We know that we have passed from death unto life, because we love the brethren. He that loveth not his brother abideth in death. Whosoever hateth his brother is a murderer: and ye know that no murderer hath eternal life abiding in him.
1 JOHN 3:14–15 KJV

God showed how much he loved us by sending his one and only Son into the world so that we might have eternal life through him.
1 JOHN 4:9 NLT

# 21

## Evil

We have felt the reality of evil in our own lives and seen it in others', too. In His Word, our holy God clearly outlines the reality of evil and shows us how to avoid the danger it presents.

You are not a God who delights in wickedness;
evil may not dwell with you.
PSALM 5:4 ESV

The LORD is watching everywhere,
keeping his eye on both the evil and the good.
PROVERBS 15:3 NLT

*God judged it better to bring good out
of evil than to suffer no evil to exist.*
SAINT AUGUSTINE

The serpent said to the woman, "You surely will not die! For God
knows that in the day you eat from it your eyes will be opened,
and you will be like God, knowing good and evil." When the
woman saw that the tree was good for food, and that it was a
delight to the eyes, and that the tree was desirable to make one
wise, she took from its fruit and ate; and she gave also to her
husband with her, and he ate.
GENESIS 3:4–6 NASB

*We can be thankful that God does not remove all evil right now.
If He did, would He not remove you? Suppose He said,
"Okay, I will do just as you request. I will take away all evil
right this minute!" Do you think that you would be spared?*
JIM ELLIFF

And I know that nothing good lives in me, that is, in my sinful
nature. I want to do what is right, but I can't. I want to do what
is good, but I don't. I don't want to do what is wrong, but I do it
anyway. But if I do what I don't want to do, I am not really the
one doing wrong; it is sin living in me that does it.
ROMANS 7:18–20 NLT

That which proceeds out of the man, that is what defiles the man. For from within, out of the heart of men, proceed the evil thoughts, fornications, thefts, murders, adulteries, deeds of coveting and wickedness, as well as deceit, sensuality, envy, slander, pride and foolishness.

MARK 7:20–22 NASB

*The more praying there is in the world, the better the world will be;*
*the mightier the forces against evil everywhere.*

E. M. BOUNDS

For our struggle is not against flesh and blood, but against the rulers, against the powers, against the world forces of this darkness, against the spiritual forces of wickedness in the heavenly places. Therefore, take up the full armor of God, so that you will be able to resist in the evil day, and having done everything, to stand firm.

EPHESIANS 6:12–13 NASB

This is the verdict: Light has come into the world, but people loved darkness instead of light because their deeds were evil. Everyone who does evil hates the light, and will not come into the light for fear that his deeds will be exposed. But whoever lives by the truth comes into the light, so that it may be seen plainly that what they have done has been done in the sight of God.

JOHN 3:19–21 NIV

Turn your back on evil, work for the good and don't quit.
GOD loves this kind of thing, never turns away from his friends.

PSALM 37:27 MSG

*If Christ has died for me. . .I cannot trifle with the evil
that killed my best Friend. I must be holy for His sake.
How can I live in sin when He has died to save me from it?*
C. H. SPURGEON

Keep your tongue from evil and your lips from speaking deceit.
Depart from evil and do good; seek peace and pursue it.
PSALM 34:13–14 NASB

Do not fret because of those who are evil or be envious
of those who do wrong; for like the grass they will soon wither,
like green plants they will soon die away.
PSALM 37:1–3 NIV

Commit your works to the LORD and your plans will be
established. The LORD has made everything for its
own purpose, even the wicked for the day of evil.
PROVERBS 16:3–4 NASB

Even though I walk through the darkest valley, I will fear no evil,
for you are with me; your rod and your staff, they comfort me.
PSALM 23:4 NIV

For you have made the LORD, my refuge, even the Most High, your
dwelling place. No evil will befall you, nor will any plague come
near your tent. For He will give His angels charge concerning
you, to guard you in all your ways.
PSALM 91:9–11 NASB

*The person who bears and suffers evils with
meekness and silence is the sum of a Christian man.*
JOHN WESLEY

Blessed are you when people insult you, persecute you
and falsely say all kinds of evil against you because of me.
MATTHEW 5:11 NIV

But I say to you, do not resist an evil person; but whoever
slaps you on your right cheek, turn the other to him also.
MATTHEW 5:39 NASB

Repay no one evil for evil. Have regard
for good things in the sight of all men.
ROMANS 12:17 NKJV

*He who passively accepts evil is as much
involved in it as he who helps to perpetrate it.*
MARTIN LUTHER KING JR.

Set a watch, O LORD, before my mouth; keep the door of my lips.
Incline not my heart to any evil thing, to practise wicked works
with men that work iniquity: and let me not eat of their dainties.
PSALM 141:3–4 KJV

The LORD will keep you from all evil; he will keep your life.
The LORD will keep your going out and your coming
in from this time forth and forevermore.
PSALM 121:7–8 ESV

*Those who believe that evil and the world are illusions do not
actually function as if this were so. They may maintain that
all is an illusion, but if one were to push them in front of an
oncoming bus, they would quickly "warm up" to the reality idea!*
NORMAN L. GEISLER

Do not be wise in your own eyes; fear the LORD
and turn away from evil. It will be healing to your
body and refreshment to your bones.
PROVERBS 3:7–8 NASB


He who earnestly seeks good finds favor,
but trouble will come to him who seeks evil.
PROVERBS 11:27 NKJV


> *It is not only that sin consists in doing evil,*
> *but in not doing the good that we know.*
> HARRY IRONSIDE


Do not be overcome by evil, but overcome evil with good.
ROMANS 12:21 NASB


Put everything to the test. Accept what is
good and don't have anything to do with evil.
1 THESSALONIANS 5:21–22 CEV


Good people bring good things out of their hearts, but evil
people bring evil things out of their hearts. I promise you
that on the day of judgment, everyone will have to account
for every careless word they have spoken.
MATTHEW 12:35–36 CEV

# 22

## Extramarital Sex

A short version of the Bible's commands on this subject
would be, "Don't do it!" The marital relationship is
a picture of Christ and the Church, and God takes
our sexual misconduct very seriously. Whether before,
during, or after marriage, extramarital sex is not
the kind of activity Christians should engage in.

Marriage should be honored by all, and the marriage bed kept pure, for God will judge the adulterer and all the sexually immoral.
HEBREWS 13:4 NIV

*When adultery walks in,*
*everything worth having walks out.*
WOODROW KROLL

You shall not commit adultery.
EXODUS 20:14 NASB

If a man is found lying with a woman married to a husband, then both of them shall die—the man that lay with the woman, and the woman; so you shall put away the evil from Israel.
DEUTERONOMY 22:22 NKJV

If a man seduces a virgin who is not pledged to be married and sleeps with her, he must pay the bride-price, and she shall be his wife.
EXODUS 22:16 NIV

Suppose a man marries a woman, but after sleeping with her, he turns against her and publicly accuses her of shameful conduct, saying, "When I married this woman, I discovered she was not a virgin.". . . Suppose the man's accusations are true, and he can show that she was not a virgin. The woman must be taken to the door of her father's home, and there the men of the town must stone her to death, for she has committed a disgraceful crime in Israel by being promiscuous while living in her parents' home. In this way, you will purge this evil from among you.
DEUTERONOMY 22:13–14, 20–21 NLT

*The first characteristic of sexual sin is deceit. It never delivers what it promises. It offers great satisfaction but gives great disappointment. It claims to be real living but is really the way to death.*

JOHN MACARTHUR

Wisdom will protect you from the smooth talk of a sinful woman, who breaks her wedding vows and leaves the man she married when she was young.
PROVERBS 2:16–17 CEV

Now the body is not for sexual immorality but for the Lord, and the Lord for the body.
1 CORINTHIANS 6:13 NKJV

*No one has ever said that sexual purity is easy. That's why scripture calls us to flee from it. The person who entertains the idea surely and quickly falls from God's standard.*

Flee sexual immorality. Every sin that a man does is outside the body, but he who commits sexual immorality sins against his own body.
1 CORINTHIANS 6:18 NKJV

But I say to you that everyone who divorces his wife, except on the ground of sexual immorality, makes her commit adultery, and whoever marries a divorced woman commits adultery.
MATTHEW 5:32 ESV

Now the works of the flesh are evident: sexual immorality, impurity, sensuality.
GALATIANS 5:19 ESV

*The monstrosity of sexual intercourse outside marriage is that
those who indulge in it are trying to isolate one kind of union
(the sexual) from all the other kinds of union which were
intended to go along with it and make up the total union.*

C. S. LEWIS

Drink water from your own cistern, and running water from your
own well. Should your fountains be dispersed abroad, streams
of water in the streets? Let them be only your own, and not for
strangers with you. Let your fountain be blessed, and rejoice with
the wife of your youth. As a loving deer and a graceful doe,
let her breasts satisfy you at all times; and always be enraptured
with her love.
PROVERBS 5:15–19 NKJV

I say then: Walk in the Spirit, and you shall
not fulfill the lust of the flesh.
GALATIANS 5:16 NKJV

# 23
## Faith

Faith is an amazing interaction between God and humans.
Our Lord calls us to trust, and through the salvation He
offers in Jesus, we believe and begin a life journey of faith.

Trust in the LORD with all thine heart;
and lean not unto thine own understanding.
PROVERBS 3:5 KJV

It is by grace you have been saved, through faith—
and this not from yourselves, it is the gift of God—
not by works, so that no one can boast.
EPHESIANS 2:8–9 NIV

Therefore, since we have been justified through faith, we have
peace with God through our Lord Jesus Christ, through whom
we have gained access by faith into this grace in which we now
stand. And we boast in the hope of the glory of God.
ROMANS 5:1–2 NIV

But that no one is justified by the law in the sight
of God is evident, for "the just shall live by faith."
GALATIANS 3:11 NKJV

*The beautiful thing about this adventure called faith
is that we can count on Him never to lead us astray.*
CHUCK SWINDOLL

Faith comes from hearing the message, and the
message is heard through the word about Christ.
ROMANS 10:17 NIV

Love the LORD, all his faithful people! The LORD preserves those
who are true to him, but the proud he pays back in full.
PSALM 31:23 NIV

*Faith is two empty hands held open to receive all of the Lord.*
ALAN REDPATH

Let love and faithfulness never leave you; bind them
around your neck, write them on the tablet of your heart.
PROVERBS 3:3 NIV

The apostles said to the Lord, "Increase our faith!" And the
Lord said, "If you had faith like a mustard seed, you would
say to this mulberry tree, 'Be uprooted and be planted
in the sea'; and it would obey you."
LUKE 17:5–6 NASB

> *What though my body run to dust?*
> *Faith cleaves unto it, counting ev'ry grain*
> *With an exact and most particular trust.*
> GEORGE HERBERT

You cannot make God accept you because of something you do.
God accepts sinners only because they have faith in him.
ROMANS 4:5 CEV

But now apart from the law, the righteousness of God has been
made known, to which the Law and the Prophets testify. This
righteousness is given through faith in Jesus Christ to all who
believe. There is no difference between Jew and Gentile, for all have
sinned and fall short of the glory of God, and are justified freely by
his grace through the redemption that came by Christ Jesus.
ROMANS 3:21–24 NIV

We who are Jews by birth and not sinful Gentiles know that a
man is not justified by the works of the law, but by faith in Jesus
Christ. So we, too, have put our faith in Christ Jesus that we may
be justified by faith in Christ and not by the works of the law,
because by the works of the law no one will be justified.
GALATIANS 2:15–16 NIV

*Faith is to believe what you do not yet see;*
*the reward for this faith is to see what you believe.*
SAINT AUGUSTINE

For we live by believing and not by seeing.
2 CORINTHIANS 5:7 NLT

I have been crucified with Christ; and it is no longer I who live,
but Christ lives in me; and the life which I now live in the flesh I
live by faith in the Son of God, who loved me and gave Himself
up for me.
GALATIANS 2:20 NASB

*A true faith in Jesus Christ will not suffer us to be idle.*
*No, it is an active, lively, restless principle; it fills the heart,*
*so that it cannot be easy till it is doing something for Jesus Christ.*
GEORGE WHITEFIELD

Even so faith, if it has no works, is dead, being by itself.
JAMES 2:17 NASB

Don't let anyone look down on you because you are young,
but set an example for the believers in speech, in conduct,
in love, in faith and in purity.
1 TIMOTHY 4:12 NIV

Watch, stand fast in the faith, be brave, be strong.
1 CORINTHIANS 16:13 NKJV

*Temptation exercises our faith and teaches us to pray.*
A. B. SIMPSON

# 24
## False Teaching

We know false teaching is out there, but how
can we identify it and avoid wrong theology?
When we know God's Word well, false teaching
will jump out at us. Anything that does not
agree with scripture is in the wrong.

Then the LORD said to me, "The prophets are prophesying falsehood in My name. I have neither sent them nor commanded them nor spoken to them; they are prophesying to you a false vision, divination, futility and the deception of their own minds. Therefore thus says the LORD concerning the prophets who are prophesying in My name, although it was not I who sent them—yet they keep saying, 'There will be no sword or famine in this land'—by sword and famine those prophets shall meet their end!"
JEREMIAH 14:14–15 NASB

> It is a remarkable fact that all the heresies which have arisen in the Christian Church have had a decided tendency to "dishonor God and to flatter man."
> C. H. SPURGEON

When a prophet speaks in the name of the LORD, if the thing does not come about or come true, that is the thing which the LORD has not spoken. The prophet has spoken it presumptuously; you shall not be afraid of him.
DEUTERONOMY 18:22 NASB

What profit is the idol when its maker has carved it, or an image, a teacher of falsehood? For its maker trusts in his own handiwork when he fashions speechless idols.
HABAKKUK 2:18 NASB

> I would say much of religious heresy is the result of a misunderstanding of the basic nature of God. And once we have a proper understanding of God, then usually most of the areas of our life coincide with who God is and what He desires for each one of us.
> JOSH MCDOWELL

There were also false prophets in Israel, just as there will be false teachers among you. They will cleverly teach destructive heresies and even deny the Master who bought them. In this way, they will bring sudden destruction on themselves. Many will follow their evil teaching and shameful immorality. And because of these teachers, the way of truth will be slandered. In their greed they will make up clever lies to get hold of your money. But God condemned them long ago, and their destruction will not be delayed.

2 PETER 2:1–3 NLT

Dear friends, do not believe every spirit, but test the spirits to see whether they are from God, because many false prophets have gone out into the world. This is how you can recognize the Spirit of God: Every spirit that acknowledges that Jesus Christ has come in the flesh is from God.

1 JOHN 4:1–2 NIV

*Compare scripture with scripture. False doctrines,*
*like false witnesses, agree not among themselves.*
WILLIAM GURNALL

Anyone who teaches something different disagrees with the correct and godly teaching of our Lord Jesus Christ. Those people who disagree are proud of themselves, but they don't really know a thing. Their minds are sick, and they like to argue over words. They cause jealousy, disagreements, unkind words, evil suspicions, and nasty quarrels. They have wicked minds and have missed out on the truth.

1 TIMOTHY 6:3–5 CEV

Now if Christ is preached that He has been raised
from the dead, how do some among you say that
there is no resurrection of the dead? But if there is no
resurrection of the dead, then Christ is not risen.
And if Christ is not risen, then our preaching is empty
and your faith is also empty.
1 CORINTHIANS 15:12–14 NKJV

> *My principal method for defeating error and heresy is by
> establishing the truth. One purposes to fill a bushel with tares;
> but if I can fill it first with wheat, I may defy his attempts.*
> JOHN NEWTON

We must stop acting like children. We must not let deceitful
people trick us by their false teachings, which are like winds
that toss us around from place to place.
EPHESIANS 4:14 CEV

Then if anyone tells you, "Look, here is the Messiah," or "There
he is," don't believe it. For false messiahs and false prophets
will rise up and perform signs and wonders so as to deceive,
if possible, even God's chosen ones. Watch out! I have warned
you about this ahead of time!
MARK 13:21–23 NLT

I know your deeds and your toil and perseverance,
and that you cannot tolerate evil men, and you put
to the test those who call themselves apostles,
and they are not, and you found them to be false.
REVELATION 2:2 NASB

# 25

## Family

The family is a God-designed institution that both reflects His love through marriage and provides a haven for raising children. So, naturally, God gives us plenty of information on how to have a happy one.

Honor your father and your mother, so that you may
live long in the land the LORD your God is giving you.
EXODUS 20:12 NIV

Then the LORD God made a woman from the rib he had taken
out of the man, and he brought her to the man. The man said,
"This is now bone of my bones and flesh of my flesh; she shall
be called 'woman,' for she was taken out of man." That is why a
man leaves his father and mother and is united to his wife, and
they become one flesh.
GENESIS 2:22–24 NIV

> *There is no more lovely, friendly, and charming relationship,*
> *communion, or company than a good marriage.*
> MARTIN LUTHER

A wife of noble character who can find? She is worth
far more than rubies. Her husband has full confidence
in her and lacks nothing of value. She brings him good,
not harm, all the days of her life.
PROVERBS 31:10–12 NIV

Wives, submit to your own husbands, as to the Lord. For the
husband is head of the wife, as also Christ is head of the church;
and He is the Savior of the body. Therefore, just as the church
is subject to Christ, so let the wives be to their own husbands in
everything. Husbands, love your wives, just as Christ also loved
the church and gave Himself for her.
EPHESIANS 5:22–25 NKJV

Husbands, likewise, dwell with [your wives] with understanding,
giving honor to the wife, as to the weaker vessel, and as being
heirs together of the grace of life,
that your prayers may not be hindered.
1 PETER 3:7 NKJV


Though my father and mother forsake me,
the LORD will receive me.
PSALM 27:10 NIV


*Children, remember that you are both God's child and your parents'
child. A happy family trusts not in their own abilities,
but in His ability to create good relationships.*


Children, obey your parents in the Lord,
for this is right.
EPHESIANS 6:1 NIV


Fathers, do not aggravate your children,
or they will become discouraged.
COLOSSIANS 3:21 NLT


*Most assuredly God will require an account of
the children from the parents' hands, for they are His,
and only lent to their care and keeping.*
A. W. PINK


He who spares his rod hates his son,
but he who loves him disciplines him promptly.
PROVERBS 13:24 NKJV

Children are a gift from the Lord; they are a reward from him.
PSALM 127:3 NLT

*We know the excitement of getting a present—we love to unwrap it to see what is inside. So it is with our children; they are gifts we unwrap for years as we discover the unique characters God has made them.*
CORNELIUS PLANTINGA

Sensible children bring joy to their father;
foolish children despise their mother.
PROVERBS 15:20 NLT

My son, keep your father's command,
and do not forsake the law of your mother.
PROVERBS 6:20 NKJV

Listen to your father who begot you,
and do not despise your mother when she is old.
PROVERBS 23:22 NKJV

If anyone does not provide for his relatives, and
especially for members of his household, he has
denied the faith and is worse than an unbeliever.
1 TIMOTHY 5:8 ESV

# 26

## Fear

There are two kinds of fear: fear of (or reverence for)
God and the doubtful fear that focuses on all the things
that could go wrong in our lives. Fear of God is a good
thing, because it draws us closer to Him in respect and
love. But doubtful fears show our lack of reliance on Him.

Oh, that [the Hebrews] had such a heart in them that they
would fear Me and always keep all My commandments,
that it might be well with them and with their children forever!
DEUTERONOMY 5:29 NKJV

*I have never once feared the devil,*
*but I tremble every time I enter the pulpit.*
JOHN KNOX

What does the LORD your God require of you, but to fear the LORD
your God, to walk in all His ways and to love Him, to serve the
LORD your God with all your heart and with all your soul, and to
keep the commandments of the LORD and His statutes which I
command you today for your good?
DEUTERONOMY 10:12–13 NKJV

Yea, though I walk through the valley of the shadow
of death, I will fear no evil: for thou art with me;
thy rod and thy staff they comfort me.
PSALM 23:4 KJV

Though a host encamp against me, my heart will not fear;
though war arise against me, in spite of this I shall be confident.
PSALM 27:3 NASB

I sought the LORD, and He heard me,
and delivered me from all my fears.
PSALM 34:4 NKJV

*Faith, which is trust, and fear are opposite poles. If a man*
*has the one, he can scarcely have the other in vigorous operation.*
ALEXANDER MACLAREN

God is our refuge and strength, always ready to help in times of trouble. So we will not fear when earthquakes come and the mountains crumble into the sea. Let the oceans roar and foam. Let the mountains tremble as the waters surge!
PSALM 46:1–3 NLT

*Are you facing fear today?. . . At times all of us experience fear. But don't allow fear to keep you from being used by God. He has kept you thus far; trust Him for the rest of the way.*
WOODROW KROLL

Many. . .are pursuing and attacking me, but even when I am afraid, I keep on trusting you. I praise your promises! I trust you and am not afraid. No one can harm me.
PSALM 56:2–4 CEV

Do not fear those who kill the body but cannot kill the soul. But rather fear Him who is able to destroy both soul and body in hell. Are not two sparrows sold for a copper coin? And not one of them falls to the ground apart from your Father's will. But the very hairs of your head are all numbered. Do not fear therefore; you are of more value than many sparrows.
MATTHEW 10:28–31 NKJV

My little group of disciples, don't be afraid! Your Father wants to give you the kingdom. Sell what you have and give the money to the poor. Make yourselves moneybags that never wear out. Make sure your treasure is safe in heaven, where thieves cannot steal it and moths cannot destroy it.
LUKE 12:32–33 CEV

For all who are led by the Spirit of God are children of God.
So you have not received a spirit that makes you fearful slaves.
Instead, you received God's Spirit when he adopted you as his
own children. Now we call him, "Abba, Father."
ROMANS 8:14–15 NLT

> *Fear is born of Satan, and if we would only*
> *take time to think a moment we would see that*
> *everything Satan says is founded upon a falsehood.*
> A. B. SIMPSON

For God has not given us a spirit of fear,
but of power and of love and of a sound mind.
2 TIMOTHY 1:7 NKJV

By faith [Moses] forsook Egypt, not fearing the wrath of the king;
for he endured as seeing Him who is invisible.
HEBREWS 11:27 NKJV

Keep your lives free from the love of money and be content with
what you have, because God has said, "Never will I leave you;
never will I forsake you." So we say with confidence, "The Lord is
my helper; I will not be afraid. What can mere mortals do to me?"
HEBREWS 13:5–6 NIV

There is no fear in love; but perfect love casts out fear,
because fear involves punishment, and the one
who fears is not perfected in love.
1 JOHN 4:18 NASB

> *When a man has quietly made up his mind that*
> *there is nothing he cannot endure, his fears leave him.*
> GROVE PATTERSON

# 27

## Following God

Following God is a lifetime commitment for the
Christian, and it will fill our lives to the brim.
It takes our whole lives to follow Jesus well.

And now, Israel, what does the LORD your God ask of you but to fear the LORD your God, to walk in obedience to him, to love him, to serve the LORD your God with all your heart and with all your soul, and to observe the LORD's commands and decrees that I am giving you today for your own good?
DEUTERONOMY 10:12–13 NIV

God looks down from heaven on all mankind to see if there are any who understand, any who seek God.
PSALM 53:2 NIV

*What were we made for? To know God. What aim should we have in life? To know God. What is the eternal life that Jesus gives? To know God. What is the best thing in life? To know God. What in humans gives God most pleasure? Knowledge of Himself.*
J. I. PACKER

Then Jesus spoke to them again, saying, "I am the light of the world. He who follows Me shall not walk in darkness, but have the light of life."
JOHN 8:12 NKJV

Those who think they know something do not yet know as they ought to know. But whoever loves God is known by God.
1 CORINTHIANS 8:2–3 NIV

*The rule that governs my life is this: Anything that dims my vision of Christ, or takes away my taste for Bible study, or cramps my prayer life, or makes Christian work difficult, is wrong for me, and I must, as a Christian, turn away from it.*
J. WILBUR CHAPMAN

And thou shalt love the Lord thy God with all thy heart,
and with all thy soul, and with all thy mind, and with all thy
strength: this is the first commandment.
MARK 12:30 KJV

But now that you have come to know God, or rather to
be known by God, how can you turn back again to the
weak and worthless elementary principles of the world,
whose slaves you want to be once more?
GALATIANS 4:9 ESV

> *The Holy Spirit makes a man a Christian, and if he is a*
> *Christian through the work of the Holy Spirit, that same*
> *Spirit draws him to other Christians in the church.*
> *An individual Christian is not Christian at all.*
> R. BROKHOFF

If someone says, "I love God," and hates his brother, he is a liar;
for he who does not love his brother whom he has seen, how can
he love God whom he has not seen? And this commandment we
have from Him: that he who loves God must love his brother also.
1 JOHN 4:20–21 NKJV

But if we live in the light, as God does, we share in life with each
other. And the blood of his Son Jesus washes all our sins away.
1 JOHN 1:7 CEV

> *If I, an earthly father, can know such a sensation of pleasure in the*
> *well-being of my son, surely that gives an inkling of how our*
> *heavenly Father feels when we please Him. If we could only*
> *grasp and be grasped by this, our lives would be revolutionized.*
> ALISTAIR BEGG

You shall follow the Lord your God and fear Him;
and you shall keep His commandments, listen to
His voice, serve Him, and cling to Him.
Deuteronomy 13:4 NASB

You have accepted Christ Jesus as your Lord.
Now keep on following him.
Colossians 2:6 CEV

So I say, walk by the Spirit, and you
will not gratify the desires of the flesh.
Galatians 5:16 NIV

Walk in love, as Christ also hath loved us, and hath
given himself for us an offering and a sacrifice to
God for a sweetsmelling savour.
Ephesians 5:2 KJV

We are his workmanship, created in Christ Jesus
unto good works, which God hath before ordained
that we should walk in them.
Ephesians 2:10 KJV

> *The Christian ideal has not been tried and found wanting.*
> *It has been found difficult and left untried.*
>
> G. K. Chesterton

# 28

## Forgiveness

Forgiveness is a huge part of the Christian life.
God has forgiven us for our sins, and we in turn are
to forgive others, with the help of His Spirit.

Who is a God like you, who pardons sin and forgives the
transgression of the remnant of his inheritance? You do not
stay angry forever but delight to show mercy. You will again
have compassion on us; you will tread our sins underfoot
and hurl all our iniquities into the depths of the sea.
MICAH 7:18–19 NIV

The LORD is slow to anger, abounding in love and forgiving
sin and rebellion. Yet he does not leave the guilty unpunished;
he punishes the children for the sin of the parents
to the third and fourth generation.
NUMBERS 14:18 NIV

*If we are not humbled by the greatness of God's forgiveness,
we need to question whether we have a relationship with Him or not.*

You are a forgiving God, gracious and compassionate,
slow to anger and abounding in love.
NEHEMIAH 9:17 NIV

If my people, which are called by my name, shall humble
themselves, and pray, and seek my face, and turn from
their wicked ways; then will I hear from heaven,
and will forgive their sin, and will heal their land.
2 CHRONICLES 7:14 KJV

He who is not with Me is against Me; and he who does
not gather with Me scatters. Therefore I say to you,
any sin and blasphemy shall be forgiven people,
but blasphemy against the Spirit shall not be forgiven.
MATTHEW 12:30–31 NASB

Blessed is the one whose transgressions
are forgiven, whose sins are covered.
PSALM 32:1 NIV

*God forgave us without any merit on our part; therefore we*
*must forgive others, whether or not we think they merit it.*
LEHMAN STRAUSS

Bless the LORD, O my soul, and forget not all His benefits:
who forgives all your iniquities, who heals all your diseases,
who redeems your life from destruction, who crowns you with
lovingkindness and tender mercies.
PSALM 103:2–4 NKJV

If we confess our sins, he is faithful and just and will
forgive us our sins and purify us from all unrighteousness.
1 JOHN 1:9 NIV

For Your name's sake, O LORD, pardon my iniquity, for it is great.
PSALM 25:11 NKJV

If you forgive other people when they sin against you, your
heavenly Father will also forgive you. But if you do not forgive
others their sins, your Father will not forgive your sins.
MATTHEW 6:14–15 NIV

*We need not climb up into heaven to see whether our sins are forgiven:*
*let us look into our hearts and see if we can forgive others.*
*If we can, we need not doubt but God has forgiven us.*
THOMAS WATSON

Then Peter came to him and asked, "Lord, how often should I forgive someone who sins against me? Seven times?" "No, not seven times," Jesus replied, "but seventy times seven!"
MATTHEW 18:21–22 NLT

*Forgiveness is an act of the will, and the will can function regardless of the temperature of the heart.*
CORRIE TEN BOOM

And when you stand praying, if you hold anything against anyone, forgive them, so that your Father in heaven may forgive you your sins.
MARK 11:25 NIV

Take heed to yourselves. If your brother sins against you, rebuke him; and if he repents, forgive him. And if he sins against you seven times in a day, and seven times in a day returns to you, saying, "I repent," you shall forgive him.
LUKE 17:3–4 NKJV

*A Christian will find it cheaper to pardon than resent. Forgiveness saves the expense of anger, the cost of hatred, the waste of spirits.*
HANNAH MORE

When people sin, you should forgive and comfort them, so they won't give up in despair. You should make them sure of your love for them.
2 CORINTHIANS 2:7–8 CEV

# 29

## Friendship

God offers His people advice on their friendships, which
are an important part of spiritual life. Our friendships,
and how we treat our friends, can tell a lot about our faith.
We need to choose our friends wisely and treat them well.

The righteous choose their friends carefully,
but the way of the wicked leads them astray.
PROVERBS 12:26 NIV

A friend loves at all times, and a brother is born for adversity.
PROVERBS 17:17 NASB

*If I do not give a friend the benefit of the doubt,
but put the worst construction instead of the best on what
is said or done, then I know nothing of Calvary's love.*
AMY CARMICHAEL

Whoever covers an offense seeks love, but he
who repeats a matter separates close friends.
PROVERBS 17:9 ESV

Never abandon a friend—either yours or your father's.
When disaster strikes, you won't have to ask your
brother for assistance. It's better to go to a neighbor
than to a brother who lives far away.
PROVERBS 27:10 NLT

One who has unreliable friends soon comes to ruin,
but there is a friend who sticks closer than a brother.
PROVERBS 18:24 NIV

The pleasantness of a friend springs from their heartfelt advice.
PROVERBS 27:9 NIV

You can trust a friend who corrects you,
but kisses from an enemy are nothing but lies.
PROVERBS 27:6 CEV

The poor are despised even by their neighbors,
while the rich have many "friends."
PROVERBS 14:20 NLT

*You may depend upon it that he is a good man whose intimate
friends are all good, and whose enemies are decidedly bad.*
JOHANN KASPAR LAVATER

Don't make friends with anyone who has a bad temper.
PROVERBS 22:24 CEV

And I tell you, make friends for yourselves by
means of unrighteous wealth, so that when it
fails they may receive you into the eternal dwellings.
LUKE 16:9 ESV

*Some friends are not worth having: the kind who deceive us and
lead us astray. Friendships should sharpen faith, not destroy it.*

Beware of your friends; do not trust anyone in your clan. For
every one of them is a deceiver, and every friend a slanderer.
Friend deceives friend, and no one speaks the truth. They have
taught their tongues to lie; they weary themselves with sinning.
JEREMIAH 9:4–5 NIV

You adulterous people, don't you know that friendship with
the world means enmity against God? Therefore, anyone who
chooses to be a friend of the world becomes an enemy of God.
JAMES 4:4 NIV

*The best way to help the world is to start by loving*
*each other, not blandly, blindly, but realistically,*
*with understanding and forbearance and forgiveness.*
MADELEINE L'ENGLE

My command is this: Love each other as I have loved you.
Greater love has no one than this, to lay down one's life for
one's friends. You are my friends if you do what I command.
JOHN 15:12–14 NIV

I no longer call you slaves, because a master doesn't
confide in his slaves. Now you are my friends,
since I have told you everything the Father told me.
JOHN 15:15 NLT

*He is your friend who pushes you nearer to God.*
ABRAHAM KUYPER

I am a friend to anyone who fears you—
anyone who obeys your commandments.
PSALM 119:63 NLT

# 30
## Giving

Though we think of giving in financial terms, God doesn't. He calls on us to live generously, not just giving our finances or our goods but sharing our whole lives with others. Whether it is forgiveness or a good meal, we are to withhold nothing from others in need.

Give to him who asks you, and from him
who wants to borrow from you do not turn away.
MATTHEW 5:42 NKJV

Jesus said to him, "If you wish to be complete, go and
sell your possessions and give to the poor, and you
will have treasure in heaven; and come, follow Me."
MATTHEW 19:21 NASB

All must give as they are able, according to
the blessings given to them by the LORD your God
DEUTERONOMY 16:17 NLT

*The most obvious lesson in Christ's teaching is that there is no
happiness in having or getting anything, but only in giving.*
HENRY DRUMMOND

Those who give to the poor will lack nothing, but those
who close their eyes to them receives many curses.
PROVERBS 28:27 NIV

The generous soul will be made rich,
and he who waters will also be watered himself.
PROVERBS 11:25 NKJV

The generous will themselves be blessed,
for they share their food with the poor.
PROVERBS 22:9 NIV

Be generous, and someday you will be rewarded.
ECCLESIASTES 11:1 CEV

Each of you should give what you have decided in your heart to give, not reluctantly or under compulsion, for God loves a cheerful giver. And God is able to bless you abundantly, so that in all things at all times, having all that you need, you will abound in every good work. As it is written: "They have freely scattered their gifts to the poor; their righteousness endures forever."
2 CORINTHIANS 9:7–9 NIV

[Those who fear the Lord] share freely and give generously to those in need. Their good deeds will be remembered forever. They will have influence and honor.
PSALM 112:9 NLT

*God has given us two hands—one to receive with and the other to give with. We are not cisterns made for hoarding; we are channels made for giving.*
BILLY GRAHAM

And whoever gives one of these little ones only a cup of cold water in the name of a disciple, assuredly, I say to you, he shall by no means lose his reward.
MATTHEW 10:42 NKJV

*He is no fool who gives what he cannot keep to gain what he cannot lose.*
JIM ELLIOT

Give, and it will be given to you. They will pour into your lap a good measure—pressed down, shaken together, and running over. For by your standard of measure it will be measured to you in return.
LUKE 6:38 NASB

Anyone who has been stealing must steal no longer, but must work, doing something useful with their own hands, that they may have something to share with those in need.
EPHESIANS 4:28 NIV

But Zacchaeus stood up and said to the Lord, "Look, Lord! Here and now I give half of my possessions to the poor, and if I have cheated anybody out of anything, I will pay back four times the amount."
LUKE 19:8 NIV

*The world asks, How much does he give?*
*Christ asks, Why does he give?*
JOHN RALEIGH MOTT

If I give all I possess to the poor and give over my body to hardship that I may boast, but do not have love, I gain nothing.
1 CORINTHIANS 13:3 NIV

*What makes the Dead Sea dead? Because it is all the time receiving,*
*never giving out anything. Why is it that many Christians are cold?*
*Because they are all the time receiving, never giving out anything.*
D. L. MOODY

Remember this: Whoever sows sparingly will also reap sparingly, and whoever sows generously will also reap generously.
2 CORINTHIANS 9:6 NIV

God gives seed to farmers and provides everyone with food. He will increase what you have, so that you can give even more to those in need. You will be blessed in every way, and you will be able to keep on being generous.
2 CORINTHIANS 9:10–11 CEV

# 31
## God's Love

Every page of His Word proclaims God's love for us. When humanity turned away from Him, our Lord chose to take that sin on Himself rather than accepting the broken relationship that resulted from sin. What more could He do to draw us to Himself?

For God so loved the world that He gave His only
begotten Son, that whoever believes in Him should
not perish but have everlasting life.
JOHN 3:16 NKJV

> *The Cross is the ultimate evidence that there is no length*
> *the love of God will refuse to go in effecting reconciliation.*
> R. KENT HUGHES

Then the LORD came down in the cloud and stood there with him
and proclaimed his name, the LORD. And he passed in front of
Moses, proclaiming, "The LORD, the LORD, the compassionate and
gracious God, slow to anger, abounding in love and faithfulness,
maintaining love to thousands, and forgiving wickedness, rebellion
and sin. Yet he does not leave the guilty unpunished; he punishes
the children and their children for the sin of the parents to the
third and fourth generation."
EXODUS 34:5–7 NIV

Understand, therefore, that the LORD your God is indeed God.
He is the faithful God who keeps his covenant for a thousand
generations and lavishes his unfailing love on those who
love him and obey his commands.
DEUTERONOMY 7:9 NLT

Thank GOD! He deserves your thanks. His love never quits.
Thank the God of all gods, his love never quits. Thank the
Lord of all lords. His love never quits.
PSALM 136:2 MSG

The LORD your God is with you, the Mighty Warrior who saves. He
will take great delight in you, in his love he will no longer rebuke
you, but will rejoice over you with singing.
ZEPHANIAH 3:17 NIV

The Father Himself loves you, because you have loved
Me and have believed that I came forth from the Father.
JOHN 16:27 NASB

*We keep asking, "Who am I that the Lord*
*should love me?" Instead we ought to be asking,*
*"Who are You, O my God, that You love me so much?"*
JOHN POWELL

But I am like an olive tree, thriving in the house of God.
I will always trust in God's unfailing love.
PSALM 52:8 NLT

*The cross is the lightning rod of grace that short-circuits God's wrath*
*to Christ so that only the light of His love remains for believers.*
A. W. TOZER

And hope does not put us to shame, because God's love has
been poured out into our hearts through the Holy Spirit, who has
been given to us. You see, at just the right time, when we were
still powerless, Christ died for the ungodly. Very rarely will anyone
die for a righteous person, though for a good person someone
might possibly dare to die. But God demonstrates his own love
for us in this: While we were still sinners, Christ died for us.
ROMANS 5:5–8 NIV

Nothing in all creation can separate us from God's
love for us in Christ Jesus our Lord!
ROMANS 8:39 CEV

This is love: not that we loved God, but that he loved us
and sent his Son as an atoning sacrifice for our sins.
1 JOHN 4:10 NIV

*If we comprehend what Christ has done for us, then surely out of gratitude we will strive to live "worthy" of such great love. We will strive for holiness not to make God love us but because He already does.*

PHILIP YANCEY

Therefore be imitators of God as dear children. And walk in love, as Christ also has loved us and given Himself for us, an offering and a sacrifice to God for a sweet-smelling aroma.
EPHESIANS 5:1–2 NKJV

Behold what manner of love the Father has bestowed on us, that we should be called children of God!
1 JOHN 3:1 NKJV

*When God calls a man, He does not repent of it. God does not, as many friends do, love one day, and hate another. . . . Acts of grace cannot be reversed. God blots out His people's sins, but not their names.*

THOMAS WATSON

No one has seen God at any time; if we love one another, God abides in us, and His love is perfected in us.
1 JOHN 4:12 NASB

We have come to know and have believed the love which God has for us. God is love, and the one who abides in love abides in God, and God abides in him.
1 JOHN 4:16 NASB

# 32
## God's Will

Knowing God's will is not a matter of memorizing
a few scripture verses, but of learning and living
in His Word. The verses here provide just a start
to understanding how God would have us live.

You must not have any other god but me.
EXODUS 20:3 NLT


And you must love the LORD your God with all
your heart, all your soul, and all your strength.
DEUTERONOMY 6:5 NLT


Remain in me, as I also remain in you. No branch can bear fruit
by itself; it must remain in the vine. Neither can you bear fruit
unless you remain in me. I am the vine; you are the branches.
If you remain in me and I in you, you will bear much fruit; apart
from me you can do nothing.
JOHN 15:4–5 NIV


In Him we have redemption through His blood, the forgiveness
of sins, according to the riches of His grace which He made
to abound toward us in all wisdom and prudence, having made
known to us the mystery of His will, according to His good
pleasure which He purposed in Himself, that in the dispensation
of the fullness of the times He might gather together in one
all things in Christ, both which are in heaven and which are on
earth—in Him.
EPHESIANS 1:7–10 NKJV


*We discover the will of God by a sensitive
application of scripture to our own lives.*
SINCLAIR FERGUSON


Trust in the LORD with all your heart,
and lean not on your own understanding.
PROVERBS 3:5 NKJV

Therefore, my dear friends, as you have always obeyed. . . :
continue to work out your salvation with fear and trembling,
for it is God who works in you to will and to act in order
to fulfill his good purpose.
PHILIPPIANS 2:12–13 NIV

*Abide in Jesus, the sinless One—which means, give up all of self
and its life, and dwell in God's will and rest in His strength.
This is what brings the power that does not commit sin.*
ANDREW MURRAY

And do not be conformed to this world, but be transformed by
the renewing of your mind, so that you may prove what the will
of God is, that which is good and acceptable and perfect.
ROMANS 12:2 NASB

Be very careful, then, how you live—not as unwise but as wise,
making the most of every opportunity, because the days are evil.
Therefore do not be foolish, but understand what the Lord's
will is. Do not get drunk on wine, which leads to debauchery.
Instead, be filled with the Spirit.
EPHESIANS 5:15–18 NIV

*Proceed with much prayer, and your way will be made plain.*
JOHN WESLEY

I urge, then, first of all, that petitions, prayers, intercession and
thanksgiving be made for all people—for kings and all those in
authority, that we may live peaceful and quiet lives in all godliness
and holiness. This is good, and pleases God our Savior, who wants
all people to be saved and to come to a knowledge of the truth.
1 TIMOTHY 2:1–4 NIV

*We must know that as His children, He's going to allow*
*problems even when we are in the center of His will.*
SANDY EDMONSON

Commit your works to the LORD,
and your thoughts will be established.
PROVERBS 16:3 NKJV

Be devoted to one another in brotherly love; give preference
to one another in honor; not lagging behind in diligence,
fervent in spirit, serving the Lord; rejoicing in hope,
persevering in tribulation, devoted to prayer.
ROMANS 12:10–12 NASB

God's will is for you to be holy, so stay away from all sexual sin.
1 THESSALONIANS 4:3 NLT

If you need wisdom, ask our generous God, and he
will give it to you. He will not rebuke you for asking.
JAMES 1:5 NLT

For it is God's will that by doing good you should
silence the ignorant talk of foolish people.
1 PETER 2:15 NIV

# 33
## God's Word

Without God's Word, how would we know about God? That's why it's important for us to know what it says. That Word helps us know Jesus, whom the Bible also calls the Word. Through the written Word and His Son, God has shown us the way to Himself.

By the word of God the heavens were of old, and the earth standing out of water and in the water, by which the world that then existed perished, being flooded with water.
2 PETER 3:5–6 NKJV

> *Too often, we look to the Bible as our guidebook for daily living. Of course, that's fine and even biblical. However, this collection of books we call the Holy Bible is much more than a self-help book. The divine purpose of this book is to point us to the One and Only.*
> RANDY HUNT

The Word was first, the Word present to God, God present to the Word. The Word was God, in readiness for God from day one.
JOHN 1:1–2 MSG

So the Word became human and made his home among us. He was full of unfailing love and faithfulness. And we have seen his glory, the glory of the Father's one and only Son.
JOHN 1:14 NLT

The Son is the radiance of God's glory and the exact representation of his being, sustaining all things by his powerful word. After he had provided purification for sins, he sat down at the right hand of the Majesty in heaven.
HEBREWS 1:3 NIV

The word of the LORD is right and true;
he is faithful in all he does.
PSALM 33:4 NIV

Forever, O LORD, your word is firmly fixed in the heavens.
PSALM 119:89 ESV

"Have faith in me, and you will have life-giving water
flowing from deep inside you, just as the Scriptures say."
JOHN 7:38 CEV

*The Bible cannot be understood simply by study or talent;*
*you must count only on the influence of the Holy Spirit.*
MARTIN LUTHER

Above all, you must realize that no prophecy in Scripture
ever came from the prophet's own understanding, or from
human initiative. No, those prophets were moved by the
Holy Spirit, and they spoke from God.
2 PETER 1:20–21 NLT

*The Bible is a window in this prison of hope,*
*through which we look into eternity.*
JOHN SULLIVAN DWIGHT

So get rid of all the filth and evil in your lives, and humbly accept
the word God has planted in your hearts, for it has the power to
save your souls. But don't just listen to God's word. You must do
what it says. Otherwise, you are only fooling yourselves. For if
you listen to the word and don't obey, it is like glancing at your
face in a mirror.
JAMES 1:21–23 NLT

I have written to you who are God's children because you
know the Father. I have written to you who are mature in the
faith because you know Christ, who existed from the beginning.
I have written to you who are young in the faith because you are
strong. God's word lives in your hearts, and you have won your
battle with the evil one.
1 JOHN 2:14 NLT

*Beware of reasoning about God's Word—obey it.*
OSWALD CHAMBERS

Whoever says, "I know him," but does not do what he commands
is a liar, and the truth is not in that person. But if anyone obeys
his word, love for God is truly made complete in them. This is
how we know we are in him: Whoever claims to live in him must
live as Jesus did.
1 JOHN 2:4–6 NIV

After he was raised from the dead, his disciples recalled
what he had said. Then they believed the scripture and
the words that Jesus had spoken.
JOHN 2:22 NIV

*Defend the Bible? I would just as soon defend a lion.*
*Just turn the Bible loose. It will defend itself.*
C. H. SPURGEON

But the Scripture has shut up everyone under sin,
so that the promise by faith in Jesus Christ might
be given to those who believe.
GALATIANS 3:22 NASB

All Scripture is God-breathed and is useful for teaching, rebuking,
correcting and training in righteousness, so that the servant of
God may be thoroughly equipped for every good work.
2 TIMOTHY 3:16–17 NIV

Thy word is a lamp unto my feet, and a light unto my path.
PSALM 119:105 KJV

# 34
## Grace

God has given us His unmerited favor, or grace. When we couldn't save ourselves, He did it for us, through His Son. As we recognize our need for grace and appreciate its work in us, God pours out His blessings in our lives.

And the Word became flesh, and dwelt among us,
and we saw His glory, glory as of the only begotten
from the Father, full of grace and truth.
JOHN 1:14 NASB

> *Grace is the very opposite of merit. . . . Grace is not*
> *only undeserved favor, but it is favor shown to*
> *the one who has deserved the very opposite.*
> HARRY IRONSIDE

In him we have redemption through his blood,
the forgiveness of sins, in accordance with the
riches of God's grace that he lavished on us.
EPHESIANS 1:7–8 NIV

For by grace are ye saved through faith; and that
not of yourselves: it is the gift of God.
EPHESIANS 2:8 KJV

And of His fullness we have all received, and grace for
grace. For the law was given through Moses, but grace
and truth came through Jesus Christ.
JOHN 1:16–17 NKJV

> *The Law tells me how crooked I am;*
> *Grace comes along and straightens me out.*
> D. L. MOODY

The Law came in so that the transgression would increase; but
where sin increased, grace abounded all the more, so that,
as sin reigned in death, even so grace would reign through
righteousness to eternal life through Jesus Christ our Lord.
ROMANS 5:20–21 NASB

For if, by the trespass of the one man, death reigned through that one man, how much more will those who receive God's abundant provision of grace and of the gift of righteousness reign in life through the one man, Jesus Christ!

ROMANS 5:17 NIV

For all have sinned and fall short of the glory of God, and are justified freely by his grace through the redemption that came by Christ Jesus

ROMANS 3:23–24 NIV

*If you would grow in grace, learn what grace is.*
*Taste and see that the Lord is good (see 1 Peter 2:2).*
SINCLAIR B. FERGUSON

But there is a great difference between Adam's sin and God's gracious gift. For the sin of this one man, Adam, brought death to many. But even greater is God's wonderful grace and his gift of forgiveness to many through this other man, Jesus Christ.

ROMANS 5:15 NLT

The LORD's curse is on the house of the wicked, but he blesses the home of the righteous. He mocks proud mockers but shows favor to the humble and oppressed.

PROVERBS 3:33–34 NIV

When grace is shown to the wicked, they do not learn righteousness; even in a land of uprightness they go on doing evil and regard not the majesty of the LORD.

ISAIAH 26:10 NIV

Those who cling to worthless idols turn
away from God's love for them.
JONAH 2:8 NIV


And I will pour out on the house of David and the inhabitants
of Jerusalem a spirit of grace and pleas for mercy, so that,
when they look on me, on him whom they have pierced,
they shall mourn for him, as one mourns for an only child,
and weep bitterly over him, as one weeps over a firstborn.
ZECHARIAH 12:10 ESV


*Divine grace was never slow.*
GEORGE HERBERT


And God is able to make all grace abound to you,
so that always having all sufficiency in everything,
you may have an abundance for every good deed.
2 CORINTHIANS 9:8 NASB


For sin shall not have dominion over you,
for you are not under law but under grace.
ROMANS 6:14 NKJV


But since you excel in everything—in faith, in speech, in
knowledge, in complete earnestness and in the love we have
kindled in you—see that you also excel in this grace of giving.
2 CORINTHIANS 8:7 NIV


*Grace is not a license to sin, but to*
*walk in humility in the sight of God.*
CURT MCCOMIS

# 35
## Healing

Whether it's our bodies or our spirits, we all need
God's healing touch. And God is always willing to
offer it to us. Look how often Jesus healed during His
ministry—not only hurting bodies but also souls that
had been severely damaged. When God does not choose
to heal our bodies, He has a soul lesson for us. Perhaps
that's what He's healing when we suffer physically.

See now that I myself am he! There is no god besides me.
I put to death and I bring to life, I have wounded and I will heal,
and no one can deliver out of my hand.
DEUTERONOMY 32:39 NIV

Let all that I am praise the LORD; may I never forget the good
things he does for me. He forgives all my sins and heals all my
diseases. He redeems me from death and crowns me with love
and tender mercies.
PSALM 103:2–4 NLT

Christ carried the burden of our sins. He was nailed to the cross,
so that we would stop sinning and start living right.
By his cuts and bruises you are healed.
1 PETER 2:24 CEV

> *Emotional healing is almost always a process. It takes time. There
> is a very important reason for this. Our heavenly Father is not only
> wanting to free us from the pain of past wounds, He is also desirous of
> bringing us into maturity, both spiritually and emotionally.*
> FLOYD MCCLUNG

He heals the brokenhearted and binds up their wounds.
PSALM 147:3 NASB

> *Christ is the Good Physician. There is no disease He cannot heal;
> no sin He cannot remove; no trouble He cannot help.*
> JAMES H. AUGHEY

Jesus went throughout Galilee, teaching in their synagogues,
preaching the good news of the kingdom, and healing every
disease and sickness among the people.
MATTHEW 4:23 NIV

That evening many people with demons in them were brought to Jesus. And with only a word he forced out the evil spirits and healed everyone who was sick.
MATTHEW 8:16 CEV

*Although our contemporary preoccupation is with the power to heal, we err by failing to understand the miracle of God's grace in granting the power necessary for endurance and patience.*
ALISTAIR BEGG

And suddenly, a woman who had a flow of blood for twelve years came from behind and touched the hem of His garment. For she said to herself, "If only I may touch His garment, I shall be made well." But Jesus turned around, and when He saw her He said, "Be of good cheer, daughter; your faith has made you well." And the woman was made well from that hour.
MATTHEW 9:20–22 NKJV

Jesus rebuked the demon, and it came out of the boy, and he was healed at that moment.
MATTHEW 17:18 NIV

*God is as willing to heal believers as He is to forgive unbelievers.*
T. L. OSBORN

When they got out of the boat, immediately the people recognized Him, and ran about that whole country and began to carry here and there on their pallets those who were sick, to the place they heard He was. Wherever He entered villages, or cities, or countryside, they were laying the sick in the market places, and imploring Him that they might just touch the fringe of His cloak; and as many as touched it were being cured.
MARK 6:54–56 NASB

There he found a man named Aeneas, who was paralyzed
and had been bedridden for eight years. "Aeneas," Peter said
to him, "Jesus Christ heals you. Get up and roll up your mat."
Immediately Aeneas got up. All those who lived in Lydda and
Sharon saw him and turned to the Lord.
ACTS 9:33–35 NIV

The same Spirit gives great faith to another,
and to someone else the one Spirit gives the gift of healing.
1 CORINTHIANS 12:9 NLT

And the prayer offered in faith will make the sick person well;
the Lord will raise them up. If they have sinned, they will be
forgiven. Therefore confess your sins to each other and pray for
each other so that you may be healed. The prayer of a righteous
person is powerful and effective.
JAMES 5:15–16 NIV

> *My grand point in preaching is to break the*
> *hard heart, and to heal the broken one.*
> JOHN NEWTON

I said, "Have mercy on me, LORD; heal me,
for I have sinned against you."
PSALM 41:4 NIV

Heal me, O LORD, and I shall be healed;
save me, and I shall be saved, for you are my praise.
JEREMIAH 17:14 ESV

O LORD my God, I cried unto thee, and thou hast healed me.
PSALM 30:2 KIV

# 36
## Holy Spirit

The Holy Spirit indwells us, as Christians, and makes us able to live for God in a sin-filled world. With the Spirit's guidance, God sends us on a heavenly mission on earth: to share His good news with the world. Only by living in the Spirit do we have success in our mission for our Lord.

But the Helper, the Holy Spirit, whom the Father will send
in My name, He will teach you all things, and bring to your
remembrance all things that I said to you.
JOHN 14:26 NKJV

Again Jesus said, "Peace be with you! As the Father has sent me,
I am sending you." And with that he breathed on them and said,
"Receive the Holy Spirit."
JOHN 20:21–22 NIV

I tell you that any sinful thing you do or say can be forgiven.
Even if you speak against the Son of Man, you can be forgiven.
But if you speak against the Holy Spirit, you can never be
forgiven, either in this life or in the life to come.
MATTHEW 12:32 CEV

> *Christ died to heal our relationship with God, but the
> Holy Spirit enables us to live for Him. Our relationship
> is with the Father, Son, and Holy Spirit, and in our lives,
> each works in concert with the other Persons of the Trinity.*

"If you then, being evil, know how to give good gifts to your
children, how much more will your heavenly Father give the
Holy Spirit to those who ask Him?"
LUKE 11:13 NASB

Therefore go and make disciples of all nations, baptizing them
in the name of the Father and of the Son and of the Holy Spirit,
and teaching them to obey everything I have commanded you.
And surely I am with you always, to the very end of the age.
MATTHEW 28:19–20 NIV

"When you are brought before synagogues, rulers and authorities, do not worry about how you will defend yourselves or what you will say, for the Holy Spirit will teach you at that time what you should say."
LUKE 12:11–13 NIV

And they were all filled with the Holy Spirit and began to speak in other tongues as the Spirit gave them utterance.
ACTS 2:4 ESV

*Without the Spirit of God we can do nothing. We are as ships without wind or chariots without steeds. Like branches without sap, we are withered. Like coals without fire, we are useless. As an offering without the sacrificial flame, we are unaccepted.*
C. H. SPURGEON

The church then had peace throughout Judea, Galilee, and Samaria, and it became stronger as the believers lived in the fear of the Lord. And with the encouragement of the Holy Spirit, it also grew in numbers.
ACTS 9:31 NLT

He chose me to be a servant of Christ Jesus for the Gentiles and to do the work of a priest in the service of his good news. God did this so that the Holy Spirit could make the Gentiles into a holy offering, pleasing to him.
ROMANS 15:16 CEV

*Trying to do the Lord's work in your own strength is the most confusing, exhausting, and tedious of all work. But when you are filled with the Holy Spirit, then the ministry of Jesus just flows out of you.*
CORRIE TEN BOOM

As they ministered to the Lord and fasted, the Holy Spirit said, "Now separate to Me Barnabas and Saul for the work to which I have called them."
ACTS 13:2 NKJV

Paul and his companions traveled throughout the region of Phrygia and Galatia, having been kept by the Holy Spirit from preaching the word in the province of Asia. When they came to the border of Mysia, they tried to enter Bithynia, but the Spirit of Jesus would not allow them to.
ACTS 16:6–7 NIV

*In any matter where we have questions, we have a right to ask the Holy Spirit to lead us and to expect His gentle guiding.*
CURTIS HUTSON

Now hope does not disappoint, because the love of God has been poured out in our hearts by the Holy Spirit who was given to us.
ROMANS 5:5 NKJV

Do not cast me away from Your presence and do not take Your Holy Spirit from me.
PSALM 51:11 NASB

Do you not know that your bodies are temples of the Holy Spirit, who is in you, whom you have received from God? You are not your own; you were bought at a price. Therefore honor God with your bodies.
1 CORINTHIANS 6:19–20 NIV

# 37
## Hope

Though at times we face severe trials, Christians
never have to live without hope. Our trust
is in God, who will never fail us.

Though He slay me, I will hope in Him.
JOB 13:15 NASB

No one whose hope is in you will ever be put to shame, but they
will be put to shame who are treacherous without excuse.
PSALM 25:3 NIV

*"Tribulation worketh patience; and patience, experience;*
*and experience, hope." That is the order. You cannot put*
*patience and experience into a parenthesis, and,*
*omitting them, bring hope out of tribulation.*
ALEXANDER MACLAREN

We glory in tribulations also: knowing that tribulation worketh
patience; and patience, experience; and experience, hope: and
hope maketh not ashamed; because the love of God is shed
abroad in our hearts by the Holy Ghost which is given unto us.
ROMANS 5:3–5 KJV

Lead me by your truth and teach me, for you are the
God who saves me. All day long I put my hope in you.
PSALM 25:5 NLT

*As far as the Lord is concerned, the time to stand is in*
*the darkest moment. It is when everything seems hopeless,*
*when there appears no way out, when God alone can deliver.*
DAVID WILKERSON

Why, my soul, are you downcast? Why so disturbed within me?
Put your hope in God, for I will yet praise him,
my Savior and my God.
PSALM 42:11 NIV

Hope deferred makes the heart sick,
but a dream fulfilled is a tree of life.
PROVERBS 13:12 NLT

For God alone, O my soul, wait in silence,
for my hope is from him.
PSALM 62:5 ESV

*If you have any hope, it comes from some faith in you.*
*Hope, you may say, is a bud upon the plant of faith,*
*a bud from the root of faith; the flower is joy and peace.*
GEORGE MACDONALD

Hopes placed in mortals die with them;
all the promise of their power comes to nothing.
PROVERBS 11:7 NIV

*If we go forth in our own strength, we shall faint, and utterly fall;*
*but having our hearts and our hopes in heaven, we shall be carried*
*above all difficulties, and be enabled to lay hold of the prize*
*of our high calling in Christ Jesus.*
MATTHEW HENRY

Even youths grow tired and weary, and young men stumble and
fall; but those who hope in the LORD will renew their strength.
They will soar on wings like eagles; they will run and not grow
weary, they will walk and not be faint.
ISAIAH 40:30–31 NIV

Be joyful in hope, patient in affliction, faithful in prayer.
ROMANS 12:12 NIV

I foresaw the Lord always before my face, for He is at my right
hand, that I may not be shaken. Therefore my heart rejoiced,
and my tongue was glad; moreover my flesh also will rest
in hope. For You will not leave my soul in Hades,
nor will You allow Your Holy One to see corruption.
Acts 2:25–27 NKJV

*He that lives in hope danceth without music.*
George Herbert

Even when there was no reason for hope, Abraham
kept hoping—believing that he would become the
father of many nations. For God had said to him,
"That's how many descendants you will have!"
Romans 4:18 NLT

We boast in the hope of the glory of God. Not only so, but we
also glory in our sufferings, because we know that suffering
produces perseverance; perseverance, character; and character,
hope. And hope does not put us to shame, because God's love
has been poured out into our hearts by the Holy Spirit,
who has been given to us.
Romans 5:2–5 NIV

And not only this, but also we ourselves, having the first fruits
of the Spirit, even we ourselves groan within ourselves, waiting
eagerly for our adoption as sons, the redemption of our body.
For in hope we have been saved, but hope that is seen is not
hope; for who hopes for what he already sees? But if we hope
for what we do not see, with perseverance we wait eagerly for it.
Romans 8:23–25 NASB

# 38
## Infertility

Scripture promises to bless those who follow the Word of God, but it also tells the stories of a number of women who were infertile, or barren, and eventually had children. Whether a woman has children or cannot conceive, God can bless her.

If you pay attention to these laws and are careful to follow them, then the LORD your God will keep his covenant of love with you, as he swore to your ancestors. He will love you and bless you and increase your numbers. He will bless the fruit of your womb, the crops of your land—your grain, new wine and oil—the calves of your herds and the lambs of your flocks in the land that he swore to your ancestors to give you. You will be blessed more than any other people.
DEUTERONOMY 7:12–14 NIV

> *Living in a time when the family is under attack, the real*
> *danger is idolizing the family. We hear "the family first"*
> *and may be tempted to say "amen." But Jesus will have none*
> *of this. When the family is first, God plays second fiddle.*
> WYNN KENYON

Worship the LORD your God, and his blessing will be on your food and water. I will take away sickness from among you, and none will miscarry or be barren in your land. I will give you a full life span.
EXODUS 23:25–26 NIV

Now Sarai [later called Sarah] was childless
because she was not able to conceive.
GENESIS 11:30 NIV

Sarah became pregnant and bore a son to Abraham in
his old age, at the very time God had promised him.
GENESIS 21:2 NIV

Isaac prayed to the LORD on behalf of his wife, because she was barren; and the LORD answered him and Rebekah his wife conceived.
GENESIS 25:21 NASB

*We must learn to see our circumstances through God's love,
and not God's love through our circumstances.*
UNKNOWN

When the LORD saw that Leah was unloved, he enabled
her to have children, but Rachel could not conceive.
GENESIS 29:31 NLT

Then God remembered Rachel's plight and answered her prayers
by enabling her to have children. She became pregnant and
gave birth to a son. "God has removed my disgrace," she said.
And she named him Joseph, for she said, "May the LORD add yet
another son to my family."
GENESIS 30:22–24 NLT

Now there was a certain man from Zorah, of the family of the
Danites, whose name was Manoah; and his wife was barren
and had no children. And the Angel of the LORD appeared to the
woman and said to her, "Indeed now, you are barren and have
borne no children, but you shall conceive and bear a son."
JUDGES 13:2–3 NKJV

[God] makes the barren woman abide in the house
as a joyful mother of children. Praise the LORD!
PSALM 113:9 NASB

Both of them were good people and pleased the Lord
God by obeying all that he had commanded. But they
did not have children. Elizabeth could not have any,
and both Zechariah and Elizabeth were already old.
LUKE 1:6–7 CEV

Your relative Elizabeth is also going to have a son, even though she is old. No one thought she could ever have a baby, but in three months she will have a son. Nothing is impossible for God!
LUKE 1:36–37 CEV

*Some couples who would like to have children never do.*
*That does not mean God is punishing them.*
*He simply has another plan for their lives.*

And we know that all things work together for good to them that love God, to them who are the called according to his purpose.
ROMANS 8:28 KJV

*To know that nothing hurts the godly is a matter of comfort; but to be*
*assured that all things which fall out shall cooperate for their good, that*
*their crosses shall be turned into blessings, that showers of affliction*
*water the withering root of their grace and make it flourish more;*
*this may fill their hearts with joy till they run over.*
THOMAS WATSON

# 39

## Integrity

Just as faith is not simply an outward thing, integrity
shows what a person is from the inside out. What we
really believe on the inside shows in our thoughts and
actions. But all our efforts at integrity cannot earn us
God's favor. Sometimes, as with the people of Israel
who were entering the Promised Land, He simply
pours out His favor on us, despite our failings.

I know, my God, that you test the heart
and are pleased with integrity.
1 CHRONICLES 29:17 NIV

Let the LORD judge the peoples. Vindicate me, LORD, according
to my righteousness, according to my integrity, O Most High.
PSALM 7:8 NIV

*Let your words be the genuine picture of your heart.*
JOHN WESLEY

Godliness guards the path of the blameless,
but the evil are misled by sin.
PROVERBS 13:6 NLT

May integrity and honesty protect me,
for I put my hope in you.
PSALM 25:21 NLT

*Integrity is keeping a commitment even*
*after circumstances have changed.*
DAVID JEREMIAH

Then the LORD asked Satan, "Have you noticed my servant Job?
He is the finest man in all the earth. He is blameless—a man of
complete integrity. He fears God and stays away from evil. And
he has maintained his integrity, even though you urged me to
harm him without cause."
JOB 2:3 NLT

The integrity of the upright guides them,
but the unfaithful are destroyed by their duplicity.
PROVERBS 11:3 NIV

It is not because of your righteousness or your integrity that you
are going in to take possession of their land; but on account of the
wickedness of these nations, the LORD your God will drive them
out before you, to accomplish what he swore to your fathers,
to Abraham, Isaac and Jacob. Understand, then, that it is not
because of your righteousness that the LORD your God is giving
you this good land to possess, for you are a stiff-necked people.
DEUTERONOMY 9:5–6 NIV

The bloodthirsty hate a person of
integrity and seek to kill the upright.
PROVERBS 29:10 NIV

*Integrity characterizes the entire person, not just part of him.*
*He is righteous and honest through and through.*
*He is not only that inside, but also in outer action.*
R. KENT HUGHES

In everything set them an example by doing what is good. In your
teaching show integrity, seriousness and soundness of speech
that cannot be condemned, so that those who oppose you may
be ashamed because they have nothing bad to say about us.
TITUS 2:7–8 NIV

*It is as hard a thing to maintain a sound understanding, a tender*
*conscience, a lively, gracious, heavenly spirit, and an upright life in the*
*midst of contention, as to keep your candle lighted in the greatest storms.*
RICHARD BAXTER

Now if you walk before Me as your father David walked, in integrity of heart and in uprightness, to do according to all that I have commanded you, and if you keep My statutes and My judgments, then I will establish the throne of your kingdom over Israel forever, as I promised David your father, saying, "You shall not fail to have a man on the throne of Israel."
1 KINGS 9:4–5 NKJV

By this I know that You are pleased with me, because my enemy does not shout in triumph over me. As for me, You uphold me in my integrity, and You set me in Your presence forever.
PSALM 41:11–12 NASB

# 40

## Joy

Joy is a key part of the Christian life, because
knowing God brings security and delight in the
Savior. No one experiences such joy without
an intimate relationship with Him.

Splendor and majesty are before him;
strength and joy are in his dwelling place.
1 CHRONICLES 16:27 NIV

And an angel of the Lord appeared to them, and the glory of the
Lord shone around them, and they were filled with fear. And the
angel said to them, "Fear not, for behold, I bring you good news
of great joy that will be for all the people. For unto you is born
this day in the city of David a Savior, who is Christ the Lord."
LUKE 2:9–11 ESV

> *Be merry, really merry. The life of a true Christian should
> be a perpetual jubilee, a prelude to the festivals of eternity.*
> THEOPHANE VENARD

Rejoice in the Lord always: and again I say, Rejoice.
PHILIPPIANS 4:4 KJV

You will show me the way of life, granting me the joy of your
presence and the pleasures of living with you forever.
PSALM 16:11 NLT

> *The out-and-out Christian is a joyful Christian. The half-and-half
> Christian is the kind of Christian that a great many of you are—
> little acquainted with the Lord. Why should we live halfway up the
> hill and swathed in the mists, when we might have an unclouded
> sky and a radiant sun over our heads if we would climb higher
> and walk in the light of His face?*
> ALEXANDER MACLAREN

The LORD is my strength and my shield;
my heart trusts in him, and he helps me.
My heart leaps for joy, and with my song I praise him.
PSALM 28:7 NIV

You have turned my sorrow into joyful dancing. No longer am I
sad and wearing sackcloth. I thank you from my heart, and I will
never stop singing your praises, my LORD and my God.
PSALM 30:11–12 CEV

Satisfy us in the morning with your unfailing love,
that we may sing for joy and be glad all our days.
PSALM 90:14 NIV

When anxiety was great within me,
your consolation brought me joy.
PSALM 94:19 NIV

> *Foolish talking and jesting are not the ways in which Christian*
> *cheerfulness should express itself, but rather "giving of thanks"*
> *(Ephesians 5:4). Religion is the source of joy and gladness, but its*
> *joy is expressed in a religious way, in thanksgiving and praise.*
> CHARLES HODGE

Worship the LORD with gladness.
Come before him, singing with joy.
PSALM 100:2 NLT

The hope of the righteous brings joy,
but the expectation of the wicked will perish.
PROVERBS 10:28 ESV

Light in a messenger's eyes brings joy to the heart,
and good news gives health to the bones.
PROVERBS 15:30 NIV

If you keep my commands, you will remain in my love,
just as I have kept my Father's commands and remain
in his love. I have told you this so that my joy may be
in you and that your joy may be complete.
JOHN 15:10–11 NIV

Ask [the Father], using my name, and you will receive,
and you will have abundant joy.
JOHN 16:24 NLT

*Joy is not necessarily the absence of suffering, it is the presence of God.*
SAM STORMS

But the fruit of the Spirit is love, joy, peace, longsuffering,
kindness, goodness, faithfulness, gentleness, self-control.
GALATIANS 5:22–23 NKJV

*I believe God, through His Spirit, grants us love, joy, and peace no
matter what is happening in our lives. As Christians, we shouldn't
expect our joy to always feel like happiness, but instead recognize joy as
inner security—a safeness in our life with Christ.*
JILL BRISCOE

Count it all joy, my brothers, when you meet trials
of various kinds, for you know that the testing of
your faith produces steadfastness.
JAMES 1:2–3 ESV

Let the sea roar, and all it contains; let the field exult, and all that
is in it. Then the trees of the forest will sing for joy before the
LORD; for He is coming to judge the earth. O give thanks to the
LORD, for He is good; for His lovingkindness is everlasting.
1 CHRONICLES 16:32–34 NASB

# 41
## Justice

God loves justice and calls His people to do so, too. Without it, leaders and legislatures rule badly, and individuals live confused lives that can never please Him. Our object lesson in justice is the cross, for through it, the Father exacted justice for the sins of the world. Jesus was punished for our sins, to make us right with our loving Father, who could not ignore sin yet wanted to continue a relationship with His people. We must pass justice on to others, as it has been given to us.

God presented Christ as a sacrifice of atonement, through the shedding of his blood—to be received by faith. He did this to demonstrate his righteousness, because in his forbearance he had left the sins committed beforehand unpunished—he did it to demonstrate his righteousness at the present time, so as to be just and the one who justifies those who have faith in Jesus.
ROMANS 3:25–26 NIV

*What do we have more to boast about than the cross of Christ, by which God has satisfied His love and His justice, His mercy and His holiness, and displayed it to all the world as He saves all who trust in Him?*
MARK DEVER

And He will judge the world in righteousness;
He will execute judgment for the peoples with equity.
PSALM 9:8 NASB

Your righteousness is like the mighty mountains, your justice like the ocean depths. You care for people and animals alike, O LORD.
PSALM 36:6 NLT

*When justice is divorced from morality, when rights of individuals are separated from right and wrong, the only definition you have left for justice is the right for every individual to do as he pleases. And the end of that road is anarchy and barbarism.*
JOHN PIPER

This is what the LORD Almighty said: "Administer true justice; show mercy and compassion to one another. Do not oppress the widow or the fatherless, the foreigner or the poor. Do not plot evil against each other."
ZECHARIAH 7:8–10 NIV

Let justice roll down like waters and
righteousness like an ever-flowing stream.
AMOS 5:24 NASB

Do not deny justice to your poor people in their lawsuits.
EXODUS 23:6 NIV

You shall do no injustice in judgment; you shall
not be partial to the poor nor defer to the great,
but you are to judge your neighbor fairly.
LEVITICUS 19:15 NASB

You Pharisees and teachers are show-offs, and you're in for
trouble! You give God a tenth of the spices from your garden,
such as mint, dill, and cumin. Yet you neglect the more important
matters of the Law, such as justice, mercy, and faithfulness.
These are the important things you should have done, though
you should not have left the others undone either.
MATTHEW 23:23 CEV

*The "least of my brethren" are the hungry and the lonely, not only
for food, but for the Word of God; the thirsty and the ignorant not
only for water, but also for knowledge, peace, truth, justice, and love.*
MOTHER TERESA

The LORD loves righteousness and justice;
the earth is full of his unfailing love.
PSALM 33:5 NIV

The LORD gives righteousness and justice
to all who are treated unfairly.
PSALM 103:6 NLT

*Justice and power must be brought together, so that whatever*
*is just may be powerful, and whatever is powerful may be just.*
BLAISE PASCAL

How blessed are those who keep justice,
who practice righteousness at all times!
PSALM 106:3 NASB

When justice is done, it brings joy to the
righteous but terror to evildoers.
PROVERBS 21:15 NIV

The righteous care about justice for the poor,
but the wicked have no such concern.
PROVERBS 29:7 NIV

Many seek the ruler's favor, but justice
for man comes from the LORD.
PROVERBS 29:26 NASB

Commit your way to the LORD; trust in him and he will do this:
he will make your righteous reward shine like the dawn,
your vindication like the noonday sun.
PSALM 37:5–6 NIV

# 42

## *Loneliness*

The Lord made people to have relationships with Himself
and others, and He recognizes and provides for our need
for human companionship. His best prescription for
loneliness: relationships with Himself and His people.

The Lord God said, "It is not good for the man to be alone;
I will make him a helper suitable for him."
GENESIS 2:18 NASB


I am like a desert owl of the wilderness, like an owl of the waste
places; I lie awake; I am like a lonely sparrow on the housetop.
PSALM 102:6–7 ESV


*Every time we let loneliness take over our feelings, we have lost sight*
*of that personal caring and loving Father: He is "Abba," our Papa.*
MICHAEL CARD


God places the lonely in families; he sets the
prisoners free and gives them joy. But he makes
the rebellious live in a sun-scorched land.
PSALM 68:6 NLT


For the enemy hath persecuted my soul; he hath smitten my
life down to the ground; he hath made me to dwell in darkness,
as those that have been long dead. Therefore is my spirit
overwhelmed within me; my heart within me is desolate.
I remember the days of old; I meditate on all thy works;
I muse on the work of thy hands. I stretch forth my hands
unto thee: my soul thirsteth after thee, as a thirsty land.
PSALM 143:3–6 KJV


Turn to me and be gracious to me, for I am lonely and
afflicted. The troubles of my heart are enlarged;
bring me out of my distresses. Consider my affliction
and my trouble, and forgive all my sins.
PSALM 25:16–18 ESV

*Snuggle in God's arms. When you are hurting, when you feel lonely, left out, let Him cradle you, comfort you, reassure you of His all-sufficient power and love.*

KAY ARTHUR

The LORD redeemeth the soul of his servants:
and none of them that trust in him shall be desolate.
PSALM 34:22 KJV

Since we want to become spiritually one with the Master,
we must not pursue the kind of sex that avoids commitment
and intimacy, leaving us more lonely than ever—
the kind of sex that can never "become one."
1 CORINTHIANS 6:16 MSG

The widow who is really in need and left all alone puts her hope in
God and continues night and day to pray and to ask God for help.
1 TIMOTHY 5:5 NIV

*The route to knowing God eventually passes directly through the valley of profound loneliness.*

LARRY CRABB

I tell myself, "I am finished! I can't count on the LORD to do
anything for me." Just thinking of my troubles and my lonely
wandering makes me miserable. That's all I ever think about,
and I am depressed. Then I remember something that fills
me with hope. The LORD's kindness never fails! If he had not
been merciful, we would have been destroyed.
LAMENTATIONS 3:18–22 CEV

# 43

## Loving Others

One of a Christian's greatest challenges may be to love others. People, after all, are so inconsistent. They cause us pain, even when they don't mean to. Let's face it—loving others can be a real sacrifice. But it's a sacrifice we can't avoid if we want to follow Jesus. Still, when we can't seem to obey, He helps us love the way He called us to.

A new command I give you: Love one another. As I have loved you, so you must love one another. By this everyone will know that you are my disciples, if you love one another.
JOHN 13:34–35 NIV

This is how we know what love is: Jesus Christ laid down his life for us. And we ought to lay down our lives for our brothers and sisters.
1 JOHN 3:16 NIV

My dear, dear friends, if God loved us like this, we certainly ought to love each other. No one has seen God, ever. But if we love one another, God dwells deeply within us, and his love becomes complete in us—perfect love!
1 JOHN 4:11–12 MSG

*If I belittle those whom I am called to serve, talk of their weak points in contrast perhaps with what I think of as my strong points; if I adopt a superior attitude. . .then I know nothing of Calvary love.*
AMY CARMICHAEL

And this is his command: to believe in the name of his Son, Jesus Christ, and to love one another as he commanded us.
1 JOHN 3:23 NIV

The one who loves his brother abides in the Light and there is no cause for stumbling in him.
1 JOHN 2:10 NASB

*I want the love that cannot help but love; loving, like God, for very sake of love.*
A. B. SIMPSON

Love each other with genuine affection,
and take delight in honoring each other.
ROMANS 12:10 NLT

Finally, all of you should be of one mind. Sympathize
with each other. Love each other as brothers and sisters.
Be tenderhearted, and keep a humble attitude.
1 PETER 3:8 NLT

*When anger wins, love always loses.*
WILLARD HARLEY, JR.

Be completely humble and gentle; be patient, bearing
with one another in love. Make every effort to keep the
unity of the Spirit through the bond of peace.
EPHESIANS 4:2–3 NIV

Owe no one anything, except to love each other, for the one who
loves another has fulfilled the law. For the commandments, "You
shall not commit adultery, You shall not murder, You shall not steal,
You shall not covet," and any other commandment, are summed
up in this word: "You shall love your neighbor as yourself."
ROMANS 13:8–9 ESV

For you have been called to live in freedom, my brothers and
sisters. But don't use your freedom to satisfy your sinful nature.
Instead, use your freedom to serve one another in love.
GALATIANS 5:13 NLT

*Love is an act of endless forgiveness.*
JEAN VANIER

And let us consider how to stir up one another to love and good
works, not neglecting to meet together, as is the habit of some,
but encouraging one another, and all the more as you see the
Day drawing near.
HEBREWS 10:24–25 ESV


Beloved, let us love one another, for love is from God;
and everyone who loves is born of God and knows God.
The one who does not love does not know God, for God is love.
1 JOHN 4:7–8 NASB


Make every effort to add to your faith goodness;
and to goodness, knowledge; and to knowledge, self-control
and to self-control, perseverance; and to perseverance, godliness;
and to godliness, mutual affection; and to mutual affection, love.
2 PETER 1:5–7 NIV


But if anyone has the world's goods and sees his brother in
need, yet closes his heart against him, how does God's love
abide in him?
1 JOHN 3:17 ESV

# 44
## *Lying*

Because God is constantly truthful, His people must be so, too. But sin has so warped our beings that we often find it hard to avoid exaggerating, misleading, or even outright telling falsehoods. When we take our inconsistencies in truth to the Truth Teller and ask His forgiveness, He who is "the way, the truth, and the life" (John 14:6) separates us from our sin.

God can't stomach liars; he loves the
company of those who keep their word.
PROVERBS 12:22 MSG

You destroy those who tell lies.
The bloodthirsty and deceitful you, LORD, detest.
PSALM 5:6 NIV

You reject all who stray from your decrees,
for their delusions come to nothing.
PSALM 119:118 NIV

Let the wicked be put to shame and be silent in the realm of
the dead. Let their lying lips be silenced, for with pride and
contempt they speak arrogantly against the righteous.
PSALM 31:17–18 NIV

Truthful lips endure forever,
but a lying tongue is but for a moment.
PROVERBS 12:19 ESV

A fortune made by a lying tongue is a fleeting
vapor and a deadly snare.
PROVERBS 21:6 NIV

A lying tongue hates those it crushes,
and a flattering mouth works ruin.
PROVERBS 26:28 NASB

*If you are of the truth, if you have learned the truth,
if you see the sanctity of the truth, then speak truth.
We are not called to be deceivers or liars. God is a God of truth,
and His people are called to have an enormously high standard of truth.*
R. C. SPROUL

Blessed is the man to whom the LORD does not impute iniquity,
and in whose spirit there is no deceit.
PSALM 32:2 NKJV

I call on the LORD in my distress, and he answers me. Save me,
LORD, from lying lips and from deceitful tongues. What will
he do to you, and what more besides, you deceitful tongue?
PSALM 120:1–3 NIV

*Those who deceive others, deceive themselves,*
*as they will find at last, to their cost.*
MATTHEW HENRY

He who conceals hatred has lying lips,
and he who spreads slander is a fool.
PROVERBS 10:18 NASB

Then they remembered that God was their rock, that God Most
High was their redeemer. But all they gave him was lip service;
they lied to him with their tongues. Their hearts were not
loyal to him. They did not keep his covenant.
PSALM 78:35–37 NLT

*Lying to ourselves is more deeply engrained than lying to others.*
FYODOR DOSTOEVSKY

For it is from within, out of a person's heart, that evil thoughts
come—sexual immorality, theft, murder, adultery, greed,
malice, deceit, lewdness, envy, slander, arrogance and folly.
All these evils come from inside and defile a person.
MARK 7:21–23 NIV

# 45
## Marriage

Marriage is a picture of the relationship between God
and His people. So, not surprisingly, God bans marriage
between believers and those who have no faith in Him.
The marital relationship is a very special covenant
between God and two people and must be honored by
all. Partners are to remain faithful to each other for life.

Marriage should be honored by all, and the marriage bed kept pure, for God will judge the adulterer and all the sexually immoral.
HEBREWS 13:4 NIV

> *I have known many happy marriages, but never a compatible one. The whole aim of marriage is to fight through and survive the instant when incompatibility becomes unquestionable.*
> G. K. CHESTERTON

Another thing you do: You flood the LORD's altar with tears. You weep and wail because he no longer looks with favor on your offerings or accepts them with pleasure from your hands. You ask, "Why?" It is because the LORD is the witness between you and the wife of your youth. You have been unfaithful to her, though she is your partner, the wife of your marriage covenant. Has not the one God made you? You belong to him in body and spirit. And what does the one God seek? Godly offspring. So be on your guard and do not be unfaithful to the wife of your youth.
MALACHI 2:13–15 NIV

Let your fountain be blessed, and rejoice in the wife of your youth. As a loving hind and a graceful doe, let her breasts satisfy you at all times; be exhilarated always with her love.
PROVERBS 5:18–19 NASB

> *If a child of God marries a child of the devil, said child of God is sure to have some trouble with his father-in-law.*
> UNKNOWN

Do not be unequally yoked together with unbelievers. For what fellowship has righteousness with lawlessness? And what communion has light with darkness?
2 CORINTHIANS 6:14 NKJV

*When your ears hear and your eyes see the sin, weakness, or failure of
your husband or wife, it is never an accident; it is always grace. God
loves your spouse, and He is committed to transforming him or her by his
grace, and He has chosen you to be one of His regular tools of change.*

PAUL DAVID TRIPP

Because of sexual immorality, let each man have his own wife,
and let each woman have her own husband. Let the husband
render to his wife the affection due her, and likewise also the
wife to her husband. The wife does not have authority over her
own body, but the husband does. And likewise the husband does
not have authority over his own body, but the wife does. Do not
deprive one another except with consent for a time, that you may
give yourselves to fasting and prayer; and come together again so
that Satan does not tempt you because of your lack of self-control.
1 CORINTHIANS 7:2–5 NKJV

To the woman [God] said, "I will make your pains in childbearing
very severe; with painful labor you will give birth to children.
Your desire will be for your husband, and he will rule over you."
GENESIS 3:16 NIV

Wives, submit yourselves unto your own husbands, as unto the
Lord. For the husband is the head of the wife, even as Christ
is the head of the church: and he is the savior of the body.
Therefore as the church is subject unto Christ, so let the wives be
to their own husbands in every thing. Husbands, love your wives,
even as Christ also loved the church, and gave himself for it.
EPHESIANS 5:22–25 KJV

Wives, submit yourselves unto your own husbands, as it is fit in the
Lord. Husbands, love your wives, and be not bitter against them.
COLOSSIANS 3:18–19 KJV

However, let each one of you love his wife as himself,
and let the wife see that she respects her husband.
EPHESIANS 5:33 ESV

*Sex appeal alone is the poorest basis in the world for a happy marriage.*
JOHN R. RICE

Whoever commits adultery with a woman lacks understanding;
he who does so destroys his own soul. Wounds and dishonor he
will get, and his reproach will not be wiped away. For jealousy
is a husband's fury; therefore he will not spare in the day of
vengeance. He will accept no recompense, nor will he be
appeased though you give many gifts.
PROVERBS 6:32–35 NKJV

*In marriage a man and a woman can become the best of friends,*
*knowing each other to such a depth that only God knows them better!*
*This, too, is a gift from the Creator.*
SINCLAIR FERGUSON

A worthy wife is a crown for her husband, but a disgraceful
woman is like cancer in his bones.
PROVERBS 12:4 NLT

An excellent wife, who can find? For her worth is far above
jewels. The heart of her husband trusts in her, and he will
have no lack of gain. She does him good and not evil
all the days of her life.
PROVERBS 31:10–12 NASB

*One of the great ironies of divorce is that people believe they are swapping their worn-out love relationship for something better. But in truth, marriage is the better thing.*

GARY AND BARBARA ROSBERG

But for those who are married, I have a command that comes not from me, but from the Lord. A wife must not leave her husband. But if she does leave him, let her remain single or else be reconciled to him. And the husband must not leave his wife.
1 CORINTHIANS 7:10–11 NLT

And a woman who has a husband who does not believe, if he is willing to live with her, let her not divorce him. For the unbelieving husband is sanctified by the wife, and the unbelieving wife is sanctified by the husband; otherwise your children would be unclean, but now they are holy.
1 CORINTHIANS 7:13–14 NKJV

A wife should stay married to her husband until he dies. Then she is free to marry again, but only to a man who is a follower of the Lord.
1 CORINTHIANS 7:39 CEV

# 46

## Mercy

Left to ourselves, we are engulfed by sin. But
God mercifully sent His Son to die for our every
wrong thought and deed. As we draw near to Him
in faith, our understanding of His mercy grows.
We recognize our own deep need for Him in every
corner of our lives, and we begin to respond to
His love by living mercifully with others.

God has mercy on whom he wants to have mercy,
and he hardens whom he wants to harden.
ROMANS 9:18 NIV

But in your great mercy you did not put an end
to [your rebellious people] or abandon them,
for you are a gracious and merciful God.
NEHEMIAH 9:31 NIV

Give up your crooked ways and your evil thoughts. Return to the
LORD our God. He will be merciful and forgive your sins.
ISAIAH 55:7 CEV

O people, the LORD has told you what is good,
and this is what he requires of you: to do what is right,
to love mercy, and to walk humbly with your God.
MICAH 6:8 NLT

> *If God's mercy might be overcome with*
> *our sins we should overcome it every day.*
> RICHARD SIBBES

For I desire mercy and not sacrifice, and the
knowledge of God more than burnt offerings.
HOSEA 6:6 NKJV

Once, you Gentiles were rebels against God, but when the people
of Israel rebelled against him, God was merciful to you instead.
Now they are the rebels, and God's mercy has come to you so
that they, too, will share in God's mercy. For God has imprisoned
everyone in disobedience so he could have mercy on everyone.
ROMANS 11:30–32 NLT

*Mercy is like the rainbow, which God hath set in the clouds; it never shines*
*after it is night. If we refuse mercy here, we shall have justice in eternity.*
JEREMY TAYLOR

Whoever conceals their sins does not prosper,
but the one who confesses and renounces them finds mercy.
PROVERBS 28:13 NIV

I will come into Your house in the multitude of Your mercy;
in fear of You I will worship toward Your holy temple.
PSALM 5:7 NKJV

*Heavenly Father. . .it is Thy mercy to afflict and try me with wants,*
*for by these trials I see my sins, and desire severance from them.*
PURITAN PRAYER

Remember your mercy, O LORD, and your steadfast love,
for they have been from of old.
PSALM 25:6 ESV

To you, LORD, I called; to the LORD I cried for mercy:
"What is gained if I am silenced, if I go down to the pit?
Will the dust praise you? Will it proclaim your faithfulness?". . .
You turned my wailing into dancing; you removed my sackcloth
and clothed me with joy, that my heart may sing your praises
and not be silent. LORD my God, I will praise you forever.
PSALM 30:8–9, 11–12 NIV

Have mercy on me, O God, because of your unfailing love.
Because of your great compassion, blot out the stain of my sins.
Wash me clean from my guilt. Purify me from my sin.
PSALM 51:1–2 NLT

Look upon me and be merciful to me, as Your custom is toward those who love Your name. Direct my steps by Your word, and let no iniquity have dominion over me.
PSALM 119:132–133 NKJV

> *A Christian should always remember that the value of his good works is not based on their number and excellence, but on the love of God which prompts him to do these things.*
>
> JOHN OF THE CROSS

Blessed are the merciful: for they shall obtain mercy.
MATTHEW 5:7 KJV

Therefore, I urge you, brothers and sisters, in view of God's mercy, to offer your bodies as a living sacrifice, holy and pleasing to God—this is your true and proper worship.
ROMANS 12:1 NIV

# 47
## Money

It's not always easy to remember that all we have comes from God, even our finances. Not only does He give us money, He also gives the promise that He will always provide for us. That doesn't mean we can spend uproariously, but as we follow Him, we will not lack what we need.

But remember the LORD your God, for it is he who gives you
the ability to produce wealth, and so confirms his covenant,
which he swore to your ancestors, as it is today.
DEUTERONOMY 8:18 NIV

Do not worry then, saying, "What will we eat?" or "What will
we drink?" or "What will we wear for clothing?" For the Gentiles
eagerly seek all these things; for your heavenly Father knows
that you need all these things. But seek first His kingdom and
His righteousness, and all these things will be added to you.
MATTHEW 6:31–33 NASB

Praise the LORD! How joyful are those who fear the LORD
and delight in obeying his commands. . . . They themselves
will be wealthy, and their good deeds will last forever.
PSALM 112:1, 3 NLT

> *God prospers me not to raise my standard of living,*
> *but to raise my standard of giving.*
> RANDY ALCORN

Every man shall give as he is able, according to the
blessing of the LORD your God that he has given you.
DEUTERONOMY 16:17 ESV

It is well with the man who deals generously and lends. . . .
He has distributed freely; he has given to the poor;
his righteousness endures forever; his horn is exalted in honor.
PSALM 112:5, 9 ESV

No one can serve two masters. Either you will hate the one and love the other, or you will be devoted to the one and despise the other. You cannot serve both God and money.
MATTHEW 6:24 NIV

*The real measure of our wealth is how much we should be worth if we lost our money.*
J. H. JOWETT

Those who trust in their wealth and boast in the multitude of their riches, none of them can by any means redeem his brother, nor give to God a ransom for him.
PSALM 49:6–7 NKJV

Woe to him who builds his house without righteousness and his upper rooms without justice, who uses his neighbor's services without pay and does not give him his wages.
JEREMIAH 22:13 NASB

*You say, "If I had a little more, I should be very satisfied." You make a mistake. If you are not content with what you have, you would not be satisfied if it were doubled.*
C. H. SPURGEON

For the love of money is a root of all kinds of evil. Some people, eager for money, have wandered from the faith and pierced themselves with many griefs.
1 TIMOTHY 6:10 NIV

The rich ruleth over the poor, and the borrower is servant to the lender.
PROVERBS 22:7 KJV

# 48

## Occult

Though many Christians are tempted to become involved in all kinds of divination, such as Ouija boards and tarot cards, and witchcraft and sorcery may have an allure, taking part in such things shows a clear lack of trust in God. No practitioner of evil has the power of our Lord, and none can protect us as He can. God equates involvement with the occult with other besetting sins, compares it to spiritual prostitution, and warns that those who persist in the unclean practices of the occult will not inherit His kingdom.

Let no one be found among you who sacrifices their son or daughter in the fire, who practices divination or sorcery, interprets omens, engages in witchcraft, or casts spells, or who is a medium or spiritist or who consults the dead.
DEUTERONOMY 18:10–11 NIV

*A wife who is 85 percent faithful to her husband is not faithful at all. There is no such thing as part-time loyalty to Jesus Christ.*
VANCE HAVNER

And the person who turns to mediums and familiar spirits, to prostitute himself with them, I will set My face against that person and cut him off from his people. . . . A man or a woman who is a medium, or who has familiar spirits, shall surely be put to death; they shall stone them with stones. Their blood shall be upon them.
LEVITICUS 20:6, 27 NKJV

Do not allow a sorceress to live.
EXODUS 22:18 NIV

Do not turn to mediums or necromancers; do not seek them out, and so make yourselves unclean by them: I am the LORD your God.
LEVITICUS 19:31 ESV

You shall not eat anything with the blood, nor practice divination or soothsaying.
LEVITICUS 19:26 NASB

*Those occult practitioners who cannot be reached with our words can be affected by prayer. As Christians intercede, God acts to show them the truth in an incontrovertible way.*

I expose the false prophets as liars and make fools
of fortune-tellers. I cause the wise to give bad advice,
thus proving them to be fools.
ISAIAH 44:25 NLT

I will put an end to all witchcraft,
and there will be no more fortune-tellers.
MICAH 5:12 NLT

Now the deeds of the flesh are evident, which are: immorality,
impurity, sensuality, idolatry, sorcery, enmities, strife, jealousy,
outbursts of anger, disputes, dissensions, factions, envying,
drunkenness, carousing, and things like these, of which I
forewarn you, just as I have forewarned you, that those who
practice such things will not inherit the kingdom of God.
GALATIANS 5:19–21 NASB

> It is a remarkable fact that all the heresies which have
> arisen in the Christian Church have had a decided
> tendency to dishonor God and to flatter man.
> C. H. SPURGEON

And when they say to you, "Seek those who are mediums and
wizards, who whisper and mutter," should not a people seek their
God? Should they seek the dead on behalf of the living?
ISAIAH 8:19 NKJV

# 49
## Patience

Patience is one of those Christian virtues we'd quite
honestly like to avoid. As we rush about, trying to
complete as many tasks as possible, patience gets shoved
off to one side, until God forces it on us. But we'd
be pretty terrible Christians if God never taught us
to wait patiently for His will. Our impatience would
show up in our interpersonal relationships as we tried
to make others fit in with our schedules. And imagine
a promising Christian ministry without patience.
No one would want to deal with such a minister!

Then he passed in front of Moses and called out,
"I am the Lord God. I am merciful and very patient
with my people. I show great love, and I can be trusted."
Exodus 34:6 CEV

The Lord is merciful! He is kind and patient,
and his love never fails.
Psalm 103:8 CEV

*Patience with others is Love, patience with self is*
*Hope, patience with God is Faith.*
Adel Bestavros

Do you think lightly of the riches of His kindness and
tolerance and patience, not knowing that the kindness
of God leads you to repentance?
Romans 2:4 NASB

Wait patiently for the Lord. Be brave and courageous.
Yes, wait patiently for the Lord.
Psalm 27:14 NLT

Better to be patient than powerful;
better to have self-control than to conquer a city.
Proverbs 16:32 NLT

Be still before the Lord and wait patiently for him;
do not fret when people succeed in their ways,
when they carry out their wicked schemes.
Psalm 37:7 NIV

Teach the older men to exercise self-control,
to be worthy of respect, and to live wisely.
They must have sound faith and be filled with love and patience.
TITUS 2:2 NLT

> *Teach us, O Lord, the disciplines of patience,*
> *for to wait is often harder than to work.*
> PETER MARSHALL

Rejoice in our confident hope. Be patient in trouble,
and keep on praying.
ROMANS 12:12 NLT

For whatever things were written before were written
for our learning, that we through the patience and
comfort of the Scriptures might have hope.
ROMANS 15:4 NKJV

> *Patience is a grace as difficult as it is necessary,*
> *and as hard to come by as it is precious when it is gained.*
> C. H. SPURGEON

We work wearily with our own hands to earn our living. We bless
those who curse us. We are patient with those who abuse us.
1 CORINTHIANS 4:12 NLT

Love is patient, love is kind and is not jealous;
love does not brag and is not arrogant.
1 CORINTHIANS 13:4 NASB

Be completely humble and gentle;
be patient, bearing with one another in love.
EPHESIANS 4:2 NIV


Brothers and sisters, we urge you to warn those who are lazy.
Encourage those who are timid. Take tender care of those
who are weak. Be patient with everyone.
1 THESSALONIANS 5:14 NLT


> *Biblically, waiting is not just something we have to*
> *do until we get what we want. Waiting is part*
> *of the process of becoming what God wants us to be.*
> JOHN ORTBERG


I pray that the Lord will guide you to be as
loving as God and as patient as Christ.
2 THESSALONIANS 3:5 CEV


The Lord's bond-servant must not be quarrelsome,
but be kind to all, able to teach, patient when wronged.
2 TIMOTHY 2:24 NASB


For God is pleased with you when you do what you know
is right and patiently endure unfair treatment. Of course,
you get no credit for being patient if you are beaten for doing
wrong. But if you suffer for doing good and endure it patiently,
God is pleased with you.
1 PETER 2:19–20 NLT


Through patience a ruler can be persuaded,
and a gentle tongue can break a bone.
PROVERBS 25:15 NIV

*The principle part of faith is patience.*
GEORGE MACDONALD

God's Spirit makes us loving, happy, peaceful,
patient, kind, good, faithful, gentle, and self-controlled.
GALATIANS 5:22–23 CEV

Therefore, as God's chosen people, holy and dearly loved,
clothe yourselves with compassion, kindness, humility,
gentleness and patience.
COLOSSIANS 3:12 NIV

*Endeavor to be always patient of the faults and imperfections of others,*
*for thou hast many faults and imperfections of thy own*
*that require a reciprocation of forbearance.*
THOMAS À KEMPIS

And the Scriptures give us hope and encouragement as we wait
patiently for God's promises to be fulfilled. May God, who gives
this patience and encouragement, help you live in complete
harmony with each other, as is fitting for followers of Christ Jesus.
ROMANS 15:4–5 NLT

# 50

## Peace

Much as we seek peace in our lives, we cannot find it
until we have peace with God, the source of all peace.
Real spiritual peace only comes through the Savior.

Therefore, since we have been justified by faith,
we have peace with God through our Lord Jesus Christ.
ROMANS 5:1 ESV

> *My Soul, there is a country*
> *Afar beyond the stars,*
> *Where stands a winged sentry*
> *All skillful in the wars;*
> *There, above noise and danger*
> *Sweet Peace sits, crown'd with smiles,*
> *And One born in a manger*
> *Commands the beauteous files.*
> HENRY VAUGHAN

For to us a child is born, to us a son is given, and the
government will be on his shoulders. And he will be called
Wonderful Counselor, Mighty God, Everlasting Father, Prince of
Peace. Of the greatness of his government and peace there will
be no end. He will reign on David's throne and over his kingdom,
establishing and upholding it with justice and righteousness from
that time on and forever.
ISAIAH 9:6–7 NIV

> *Peace with God does not always mean a calm time of happiness.*
> *The salvation that Jesus brought comes with a price: conflict against evil.*
> *But in the end, all who trust in Him experience the peace of eternal life.*

But whoever denies Me before men, I will also deny him before
My Father who is in heaven. Do not think that I came to bring
peace on the earth; I did not come to bring peace, but a sword.
MATTHEW 10:33–34 NASB

The Lord bless you, and keep you; the Lord make His
face shine on you, and be gracious to you; the Lord lift
up His countenance on you, and give you peace.
NUMBERS 6:24–26 NASB

For the mind set on the flesh is death,
but the mind set on the Spirit is life and peace.
ROMANS 8:6 NASB

*God cannot give us happiness and peace apart from Himself,*
*because it is not there. There is no such thing.*
C. S. LEWIS

Those who love Your law have great peace,
and nothing causes them to stumble.
PSALM 119:165 NASB

Mark the blameless man, and observe the
upright; for the future of that man is peace.
PSALM 37:37 NKJV

The Lord gives strength to his people;
the Lord blesses his people with peace.
PSALM 29:11 NIV

In peace I will lie down and sleep, for you alone,
O Lord, will keep me safe.
PSALM 4:8 NLT

*Peace is always beautiful.*
WALT WHITMAN

Depart from evil and do good; seek peace and pursue it.
PSALM 34:14 NASB

The LORD gives perfect peace to those whose faith is firm.
ISAIAH 26:3 CEV

*Peacemakers carry about with them an atmosphere*
*in which quarrels die a natural death.*
R. T. ARCHIBALD

Blessed are the peacemakers: for they
shall be called the children of God.
MATTHEW 5:9 KJV

Peace I leave with you, My peace I give to you;
not as the world gives do I give to you.
Let not your heart be troubled, neither let it be afraid.
JOHN 14:27 NKJV

If it is possible, as far as it depends on you,
live at peace with everyone.
ROMANS 12:18 NIV

Finally, brothers, rejoice. Aim for restoration, comfort
one another, agree with one another, live in peace;
and the God of love and peace will be with you.
2 CORINTHIANS 13:11 ESV

And let the peace that comes from Christ rule in your hearts.
For as members of one body you are called to live in peace.
And always be thankful.
COLOSSIANS 3:15 NLT

# 51

## Pornography

Though scripture never uses the word pornography,
clearly this kind of lust is not to be part of the Christian
lifestyle. The strength to combat this sin comes from a
life dedicated to God and empowered by His Spirit.

But I say, anyone who even looks at a woman with lust
has already committed adultery with her in his heart.
MATTHEW 5:28 NLT

*God made every one of us a sexual being, and that is good.*
*Attraction and arousal are the natural, spontaneous, God-given*
*responses to physical beauty, while lust is a deliberate act of the will.*
RICK WARREN

To keep you from the evil woman, from the flattering tongue
of a seductress. Do not lust after her beauty in your heart,
nor let her allure you with her eyelids.
PROVERBS 6:24–25 NKJV

Even so consider yourselves to be dead to sin, but alive to God
in Christ Jesus. Therefore do not let sin reign in your mortal
body so that you obey its lusts, and do not go on presenting the
members of your body to sin as instruments of unrighteousness;
but present yourselves to God as those alive from the dead,
and your members as instruments of righteousness to God.
ROMANS 6:11–13 NASB

For all that is in the world, the lust of the flesh and the lust
of the eyes and the boastful pride of life, is not from the Father,
but is from the world.
1 JOHN 2:16 NASB

*Imagination is the hotbed where this sin is too often hatched.*
*Guard your thoughts, and there will be little fear about your actions.*
J. C. RYLE

Let us walk properly as in the daytime, not in orgies and drunkenness, not in sexual immorality and sensuality, not in quarreling and jealousy. But put on the Lord Jesus Christ, and make no provision for the flesh, to gratify its desires.
ROMANS 13:13–14 ESV

So put to death the sinful, earthly things lurking within you. Have nothing to do with sexual immorality, impurity, lust, and evil desires.
COLOSSIANS 3:5 NLT

*The secret of living a life of excellence is merely a matter of thinking thoughts of excellence. Really, it's a matter of programming our minds with the kind of information that will set us free.*
CHUCK SWINDOLL

Since we want to become spiritually one with the Master, we must not pursue the kind of sex that avoids commitment and intimacy, leaving us more lonely than ever— the kind of sex that can never "become one."
1 CORINTHIANS 6:16 MSG

Flee also youthful lusts; but pursue righteousness, faith, love, peace with those who call on the Lord out of a pure heart.
2 TIMOTHY 2:22 NKJV

The world and its desires pass away, but whoever does the will of God lives forever.
1 JOHN 2:17 NIV

I say then: Walk in the Spirit, and you shall not fulfill the lust of the flesh. For the flesh lusts against the Spirit, and the Spirit against the flesh; and these are contrary to one another, so that you do not do the things that you wish.
GALATIANS 5:16–17 NKJV

Therefore, since Christ suffered in his body, arm yourselves also with the same attitude, because whoever suffers in the body is done with sin. As a result, they do not live the rest of their earthly lives for evil human desires, but rather for the will of God. For you have spent enough time in the past doing what pagans choose to do—living in debauchery, lust, drunkenness, orgies, carousing and detestable idolatry.
1 PETER 4:1–3 NIV

Let thy fountain be blessed: and rejoice with the wife of thy youth. Let her be as the loving hind and pleasant roe; let her breasts satisfy thee at all times; and be thou ravished always with her love.
PROVERBS 5:18–19 KJV

# 52

## Possessions

Though wealth and many possessions are gifts from God, they can also distract believers from the fact that all in this life is temporary. However many possessions God gives us, we need to share them generously and store up treasures in heaven.

As for every man to whom God has given riches and wealth, and given him power to eat of it, to receive his heritage and rejoice in his labor—this is the gift of God.
ECCLESIASTES 5:19 NKJV

Jesus answered, "If you want to be perfect, go, sell your possessions and give to the poor, and you will have treasure in heaven. Then come, follow me." When the young man heard this, he went away sad, because he had great wealth. Then Jesus said to his disciples, "I tell you the truth, it is hard for someone who is rich to enter the kingdom of heaven. Again I tell you, it is easier for a camel to go through the eye of a needle than for someone who is rich to enter the kingdom of God."
MATTHEW 19:21–24 NIV

The lazy do not roast any game, but the diligent feed on the riches of the hunt.
PROVERBS 12:27 NIV

> *Nothing, I am sure, has such a tendency to quench the fire of religion as the possession of money.*
> J. C. RYLE

And he said to them, "Take care, and be on your guard against all covetousness, for one's life does not consist in the abundance of his possessions."
LUKE 12:15 ESV

> *There are three conversions necessary: the conversion of the heart, mind, and the purse.*
> MARTIN LUTHER

I have seen another evil under the sun, and it weighs heavily on mankind: God gives some people wealth, possessions and honor, so that they lack nothing their hearts desire, but God does not grant them the ability to enjoy them, and strangers enjoy them instead. This is meaningless, a grievous evil.

ECCLESIASTES 6:1–2 NIV

Sell your possessions and give to those in need. This will store up treasure for you in heaven! And the purses of heaven never get old or develop holes. Your treasure will be safe; no thief can steal it and no moth can destroy it.

LUKE 12:33 NLT

Zaccheus stopped and said to the Lord, "Behold, Lord, half of my possessions I will give to the poor, and if I have defrauded anyone of anything, I will give back four times as much." And Jesus said to him, "Today salvation has come to this house, because he, too, is a son of Abraham."

LUKE 19:8–9 NASB

Everyone around was in awe—all those wonders and signs done through the apostles! And all the believers lived in a wonderful harmony, holding everything in common. They sold whatever they owned and pooled their resources so that each person's need was met.

ACTS 2:43–45 MSG

*To dispense our wealth liberally is the best way to preserve it.*
ISAAC BARROW

Now the multitude of those who believed were of one heart
and one soul; neither did anyone say that any of the things he
possessed was his own, but they had all things in common.
ACTS 4:32 NKJV

*Seek not great things for yourselves in this world, for if your garments
be too long, they will make you stumble; and one staff helps a man in
his journey, when many in his hands at once hinders him.*
WILLIAM BRIDGE

You suffered along with those who were thrown into jail, and when
all you owned was taken from you, you accepted it with joy. You
knew there were better things waiting for you that will last forever.
HEBREWS 10:34 NLT

But if anyone has the world's goods and sees his
brother in need, yet closes his heart against him,
how does God's love abide in him?
1 JOHN 3:17 ESV

If I give all I possess to the poor and give over my body to
hardship that I may boast, but have not love, I gain nothing.
1 CORINTHIANS 13:3 NIV

# 53
## Power

As we seek to nail down our busy lives, we often forget that all power comes from our Lord and no human is more powerful than He. When we bear power, we are to do so as those wielding it for Him.

Your right hand, O LORD, is majestic in power, Your right hand, O
LORD, shatters the enemy. And in the greatness of Your excellence
You overthrow those who rise up against You; You send forth
Your burning anger, and it consumes them as chaff.
EXODUS 15:6–7 NASB

Yours, LORD, is the greatness and the power and the glory
and the majesty and the splendor, for everything in heaven
and earth is yours. Yours, LORD, is the kingdom; you are
exalted as head over all. Wealth and honor come from you;
you are the ruler of all things. In your hands are strength
and power to exalt and give strength to all.
1 CHRONICLES 29:11–12 NIV

*God's power is like Himself: infinite, eternal, incomprehensible;*
*it can neither be checked, restrained, nor frustrated by the creature.*
STEPHEN CHARNOCK

Once God has spoken; twice I have heard this:
That power belongs to God; and lovingkindness is Yours,
O Lord, for You recompense a man according to his work.
PSALM 62:11–12 NASB

You have by Your power redeemed Your people,
the sons of Jacob and Joseph.
PSALM 77:15 NASB

He has shown his people the power of his works,
in giving them the inheritance of the nations.
PSALM 111:6 ESV

The Good News is about his Son. In his earthly life he was born
into King David's family line, and he was shown to be the
Son of God when he was raised from the dead by the
power of the Holy Spirit. He is Jesus Christ our Lord.
ROMANS 1:3–4 NLT

And all the people were trying to touch Him,
for power was coming from Him and healing them all.
LUKE 6:19 NASB

For since the creation of the world His invisible attributes are
clearly seen, being understood by the things that are made,
even His eternal power and Godhead, so that [those who
do not believe in Him] are without excuse.
ROMANS 1:20 NKJV

What man can live and not see death?
Can he deliver his life from the power of the grave?
PSALM 89:48 NKJV

The wise prevail through great power,
and those who have knowledge muster their strength.
PROVERBS 24:5 NIV

*If you look up into His face and say, "Yes, Lord, whatever it costs,"
at that moment He'll flood your life with His presence and power.*
ALAN REDPATH

He giveth power to the faint; and to them
that have no might he increaseth strength.
ISAIAH 40:29 KJV

*If we think of the Holy Spirit only as an impersonal power or influence, then our thought will constantly be, How can I get hold of and use the Holy Spirit; but if we think of Him in the biblical way as a divine Person, infinitely wise, infinitely holy, infinitely tender, then our thought will constantly be, How can the Holy Spirit get hold of and use me?*
R. A. TORREY

"But you will receive power when the Holy Spirit comes upon you. And you will be my witnesses, telling people about me everywhere—in Jerusalem, throughout Judea, in Samaria, and to the ends of the earth."
ACTS 1:8 NLT

I am not ashamed of the gospel, because it is the power of God that brings salvation to everyone who believes: first to the Jew, then to the Gentile.
ROMANS 1:16 NIV

*The authority by which the Christian leader leads is not power but love, not force but example, not coercion but reasoned persuasion. Leaders have power, but power is safe only in the hands of those who humble themselves to serve.*
JOHN STOTT

And with great power the apostles were giving their testimony to the resurrection of the Lord Jesus, and great grace was upon them all.
ACTS 4:33 ESV

*If you are strangers to prayer you are strangers to power.*
BILLY SUNDAY

I pray that God, the source of hope, will fill you completely with joy and peace because you trust in him. Then you will overflow with confident hope through the power of the Holy Spirit.
ROMANS 15:13 NLT

For the word of the cross is folly to those who are perishing, but to us who are being saved it is the power of God.
1 CORINTHIANS 1:18 ESV

Then will appear the sign of the Son of Man in heaven. And then all the peoples of the earth will mourn when they see the Son of Man coming on the clouds of heaven, with power and great glory.
MATTHEW 24:30 NIV

God's kingdom isn't just a lot of words. It is power.
1 CORINTHIANS 4:20 CEV

# 54
## Prayer

Prayer should be a precious thing, since it is communication with our Lord. But how often do we skimp on prayer, pushing it out of our busy lives? Prayerless Christians become weak, helpless believers. But with it we can move mountains.

The LORD detests the sacrifice of the wicked,
but he delights in the prayers of the upright.
PROVERBS 15:8 NLT


He will respond to the prayer of the destitute;
he will not despise their plea.
PSALM 102:17 NIV


Do not be anxious about anything, but in everything, by prayer
and petition, with thanksgiving, present your requests to God.
PHILIPPIANS 4:6 NIV


*Never wait for fitter time or place to talk to Him. To wait till you go to
church or to your closet is to make Him wait. He will listen as you walk.*
GEORGE MACDONALD


Pray in the Spirit at all times and on every occasion. Stay alert
and be persistent in your prayers for all believers everywhere.
EPHESIANS 6:18 NLT


Pray without ceasing.
1 THESSALONIANS 5:17 KJV


*We are too busy to pray, and so we are too busy to have power.
We have a great deal of activity, but we accomplish little;
many services but few conversions; much machinery but few results.*
R. A. TORREY


I want everyone everywhere to lift innocent hands toward heaven
and pray, without being angry or arguing with each other.
1 TIMOTHY 2:8 CEV

*The spirit of prayer is a pressing forth of the soul out of this earthly*
*life, it is a stretching with all its desire after the life of God, it is a*
*leaving, as far as it can, all its own spirit, to receive a spirit from*
*above, to be one life, one love, one spirit with Christ in God.*
WILLIAM LAW

Answer me when I call to you, O my righteous God. Give me
relief from my distress; be merciful to me and hear my prayer.
PSALM 4:1 NIV

The LORD has heard my plea; the LORD accepts my prayer.
PSALM 6:9 ESV

We worship you, Lord, and we should always pray
whenever we find out that we have sinned.
Then we won't be swept away by a raging flood.
PSALM 32:6 CEV

*If God can bring blessing from the broken body of Jesus*
*and glory from something that's as obscene as the cross,*
*He can bring blessing from my problems and my pain*
*and my unanswered prayer. I just have to trust Him.*
ANNE GRAHAM LOTZ

I am the one who has seen the afflictions that come from the
rod of the LORD's anger. . . . He has walled me in, and I cannot
escape. He has bound me in heavy chains. And though I cry and
shout, he has shut out my prayers.
LAMENTATIONS 3:1, 7–8 NLT

But I tell you to love your enemies and
pray for anyone who mistreats you.
MATTHEW 5:44 CEV

*On days when life is difficult and I feel overwhelmed, as I do*
*fairly often, it helps to remember in my prayers that all God requires*
*of me is to trust Him and be His friend. I find I can do that.*
BRUCE LARSON

Rejoice in hope, be patient in tribulation, be constant in prayer.
ROMANS 12:12 ESV

But when you pray, go into your room, close the door and pray to
your Father, who is unseen. Then your Father, who sees what is
done in secret, will reward you. And when you pray, do not keep
on babbling like pagans, for they think they will be heard because
of their many words. Do not be like them, for your Father knows
what you need before you ask him.
MATTHEW 6:6–8 NIV

This, then, is how you should pray: "Our Father in heaven,
hallowed be your name, your kingdom come, your will be done,
on earth as it is in heaven. Give us today our daily bread. And
forgive us our debts, as we also have forgiven our debtors. And
lead us not into temptation, but deliver us from the evil one."
MATTHEW 6:9–13 NIV

And all things you ask in prayer, believing, you will receive.
MATTHEW 21:22 NASB

*Invariable "success" in prayer would not prove the Christian doctrine*
*at all. It would prove something more like magic—a power in*
*certain human beings to control, or compel, the course of nature.*
C. S. LEWIS

# 55

## Pride

Pride is a dangerous sin that separates us from
our all-powerful God. When we focus on our own
frail "power," we cannot truly see Him as Lord.

I, the LORD, will punish the world for its evil and the
wicked for their sin. I will crush the arrogance of the
proud and humble the pride of the mighty.
ISAIAH 13:11 NLT


The LORD will tear down the house of the proud,
but He will establish the boundary of the widow.
PROVERBS 15:25 NASB


*There is something within the human spirit that wants to resist the
thought of weakness. Many times this is nothing more than our human
pride at work. Just as weakness carries a great potential for strength,
pride carries an equally great potential for defeat.*
CHARLES STANLEY


The eyes of the arrogant will be humbled and human pride
brought low; the LORD alone will be exalted in [the day of the Lord].
ISAIAH 2:11 NIV


The fear of the LORD is to hate evil; pride and arrogance
and the evil way and the perverse mouth I hate.
PROVERBS 8:13 NKJV


How blessed is the man who has made the LORD his trust, and has
not turned to the proud, nor to those who lapse into falsehood.
PSALM 40:4 NASB


Believers in humble circumstances ought to take pride in their
high position. But the rich should take pride in their humiliation—
since they will pass away like a wild flower.
JAMES 1:9–10 NIV

*Pride is to character like the attic to the house—*
*the highest part, and generally the most empty.*
SYDNEY HOWARD GAY

Too much pride can put you to shame.
It's wiser to be humble.
PROVERBS 11:2 CEV

Finishing is better than starting.
Patience is better than pride.
ECCLESIASTES 7:8 NLT

Where there is strife, there is pride,
but wisdom is found in those who take advice.
PROVERBS 13:10 NIV

*If I had only one sermon to preach it*
*would be a sermon against pride.*
G. K. CHESTERTON

Pride goes before destruction, and haughtiness before a fall.
PROVERBS 16:18 NLT

In his pride the wicked man does not seek him;
in all his thoughts there is no room for God.
PSALM 10:4 NIV

Mockers are proud and haughty;
they act with boundless arrogance.
PROVERBS 21:24 NLT

# 56

## Salvation

Until we recognize our sin, we remain unconvinced we've done anything wrong. But when God's Spirit grabs hold of our lives, we begin to understand our need for salvation and the only One who can provide it. The theme of God's salvation appears in the Old Testament, but it comes to fruition in the life, death, and resurrection of His Son, Jesus. Through Him, people are saved as they answer His call to redemption.

Jesus is "the stone you builders rejected, which has become the capstone." Salvation is found in no one else, for there is no other name under heaven given to mankind by which we must be saved.
ACTS 4:11–12 NIV

The LORD is my strength and song, and He has become
my salvation; He is my God, and I will praise Him;
my father's God, and I will exalt Him.
EXODUS 15:2 NKJV

The LORD has made known His salvation;
He has revealed His righteousness in the sight of the nations.
PSALM 98:2 NASB

For the LORD takes delight in his people;
he crowns the humble with victory.
PSALM 149:4 NIV

> *Safety does not depend on our conception of the absence of danger.*
> *Safety is found in God's presence, in the center of His perfect will.*
> T. J. BACH

My God is my rock, in whom I find protection. He is my shield,
the power that saves me, and my place of safety. He is my
refuge, my savior, the one who saves me from violence.
2 SAMUEL 22:3 NLT

I trust in your unfailing love; my heart rejoices in your salvation.
PSALM 13:5 NIV

*The only thing of our very own which we contribute to*
*our salvation is the sin which makes it necessary.*
WILLIAM TEMPLE

Salvation is far from the wicked,
for they do not seek Your statutes.
PSALM 119:155 NKJV

For I am not ashamed of the gospel, for it is the power
of God for salvation to everyone who believes,
to the Jew first and also to the Greek.
ROMANS 1:16 ESV

As God's partners, we beg you not to accept this marvelous gift
of God's kindness and then ignore it. For God says, "At just the
right time, I heard you. On the day of salvation, I helped you."
Indeed, the "right time" is now. Today is the day of salvation.
2 CORINTHIANS 6:1–2 NLT

And you also were included in Christ when you heard the word
of truth, the gospel of your salvation. When you believed, you
were marked in him with a seal, the promised Holy Spirit, who is
a deposit guaranteeing our inheritance until the redemption of
those who are God's possession—to the praise of his glory.
EPHESIANS 1:13–14 NIV

*Jesus didn't save you so you could cruise to heaven in a luxury liner.*
*He wants you to be useful in His kingdom! The moment you got saved,*
*He enrolled you in His school—the school of suffering and affliction.*
DAVID WILKERSON

Therefore, my beloved, as you have always obeyed, not as in my presence only, but now much more in my absence, work out your own salvation with fear and trembling; for it is God who works in you both to will and to do for His good pleasure.

PHILIPPIANS 2:12–13 NKJV

Like newborn babies, crave pure spiritual milk,
so that by it you may grow up in your salvation,
now that you have tasted that the Lord is good.

1 PETER 2:2–3 NIV

Lift up your eyes to the sky, then look to the earth beneath; for the sky will vanish like smoke, and the earth will wear out like a garment and its inhabitants will die in like manner; but My salvation will be forever, and My righteousness will not wane.

ISAIAH 51:6 NASB

*God is none other than the Savior of our wretchedness.*
*So we can only know God well by knowing our iniquities. . . .*
*Those who have known God without knowing their wretchedness*
*have not glorified Him, but have glorified themselves.*

BLAISE PASCAL

And inasmuch as it is appointed for men to die once and after this comes judgment, so Christ also, having been offered once to bear the sins of many, will appear a second time for salvation without reference to sin, to those who eagerly await Him.

HEBREWS 9:27–28 NASB

# 57

## Sin

Our holy God cannot tolerate sin, so since the fall
of Adam and Eve, it has separated humanity from
God. Yet our compassionate Lord did not accept that
distance and sent His Son, Jesus, as a sacrifice for our
sin. Justice was satisfied, and we were reunited with
our Lord through faith. But for believers, every day
requires that we resist sin and seek to obey our Savior.

The LORD passed before [Moses] and proclaimed, "The LORD, the LORD, a God merciful and gracious, slow to anger, and abounding in steadfast love and faithfulness, keeping steadfast love for thousands, forgiving iniquity and transgression and sin, but who will by no means clear the guilty, visiting the iniquity of the fathers on the children and the children's children, to the third and the fourth generation."
EXODUS 34:6–7 ESV

*Sin is wrong, not because of what it does to me, or my spouse, or child, or neighbor, but because it is an act of rebellion against the infinitely holy and majestic God.*
JERRY BRIDGES

Be gracious to me, O God, according to Your lovingkindness; according to the greatness of Your compassion blot out my transgressions. Wash me thoroughly from my iniquity and cleanse me from my sin. For I know my transgressions and my sin is ever before me. Against You, You only, I have sinned and done what is evil in Your sight, so that You are justified when You speak and blameless when You judge.
PSALM 51:1–4 NASB

[Jesus] himself bore our sins in his body on the tree, that we might die to sin and live to righteousness. By his wounds you have been healed.
1 PETER 2:24 ESV

The next day [John the Baptist] saw Jesus coming toward him, and said, "Behold, the Lamb of God, who takes away the sin of the world!"
JOHN 1:29 ESV

Behold, I was brought forth in iniquity,
and in sin my mother conceived me.
PSALM 51:5 NKJV

The wages of the righteous is life,
the income of the wicked, punishment.
PROVERBS 10:16 NASB

Therefore, just as sin came into the world through one man,
and death through sin, and so death spread to all men because
all sinned—for sin indeed was in the world before the law was
given, but sin is not counted where there is no law.
ROMANS 5:12–13 ESV

*Jesus was God and man in one person,*
*that God and man might be happy together again.*
GEORGE WHITFIELD

For He made Him who knew no sin to be sin for us,
that we might become the righteousness of God in Him.
2 CORINTHIANS 5:21 NKJV

Jesus replied, "I tell you the truth,
everyone who sins is a slave of sin."
JOHN 8:34 NLT

For a man's ways are before the eyes of the LORD, and he
ponders all his paths. The iniquities of the wicked ensnare him,
and he is held fast in the cords of his sin.
PROVERBS 5:21–22 ESV

We know that the Law is spiritual. But I am merely a human, and I have been sold as a slave to sin. In fact, I don't understand why I act the way I do. I don't do what I know is right. I do the things I hate. Although I don't do what I know is right, I agree that the Law is good. So I am not the one doing these evil things. The sin that lives in me is what does them. I know that my selfish desires won't let me do anything that is good. Even when I want to do right, I cannot. Instead of doing what I know is right, I do wrong.
ROMANS 7:14–19 CEV

No one who abides in him keeps on sinning; no one who keeps on sinning has either seen him or known him.
1 JOHN 3:6 ESV

When [Jesus] died, he died once to break the power of sin. But now that he lives, he lives for the glory of God. So you also should consider yourselves to be dead to the power of sin and alive to God through Christ Jesus. Do not let sin control the way you live; do not give in to sinful desires. Do not let any part of your body become an instrument of evil to serve sin. Instead, give yourselves completely to God, for you were dead, but now you have new life. So use your whole body as an instrument to do what is right for the glory of God. Sin is no longer your master, for you no longer live under the requirements of the law. Instead, you live under the freedom of God's grace.
ROMANS 6:10–14 NLT

*We must learn where our personal weaknesses lie. Once they are identified, we must be ruthless in dealing with them.*
ALISTAIR BEGG

What then? Shall we sin because we are not under law but under grace? May it never be! Do you not know that when you present yourselves to someone as slaves for obedience, you are slaves of the one whom you obey, either of sin resulting in death, or of obedience resulting in righteousness? But thanks be to God that though you were slaves of sin, you became obedient from the heart to that form of teaching to which you were committed, and having been freed from sin, you became slaves of righteousness.
ROMANS 6:15–18 NASB

But now that you have been set free from sin and have become slaves of God, the fruit you get leads to sanctification and its end, eternal life. For the wages of sin is death, but the free gift of God is eternal life in Christ Jesus our Lord.
ROMANS 6:22–23 ESV

> *After grief for sin there should be joy for forgiveness.*
> A. W. PINK

For while we were living in the flesh, our sinful passions, aroused by the law, were at work in our members to bear fruit for death. But now we are released from the law, having died to that which held us captive, so that we serve in the new way of the Spirit and not in the old way of the written code.
ROMANS 7:5–6 ESV

But each of you had better tremble and turn from your sins. Silently search your heart as you lie in bed.
PSALM 4:4 CEV

> *It does not spoil your happiness to confess your sin.*
> *The unhappiness is in not making the confession.*
> C. H. SPURGEON

Flee from sexual immorality. All other sins a person
commits are outside the body, but whoever sins
sexually, sins against their own body.
1 CORINTHIANS 6:18 NIV

And if Christ is in you, the body is dead because of sin,
but the Spirit is life because of righteousness.
ROMANS 8:10 NKJV

If we confess our sins, he is faithful and just to forgive
us our sins, and to cleanse us from all unrighteousness.
1 JOHN 1:9 KJV

I have hidden your word in my heart that I might not sin against you.
PSALM 119:11 NIV

Therefore, dear brothers and sisters, you have no obligation to
do what your sinful nature urges you to do. For if you live by its
dictates, you will die. But if through the power of the Spirit you
put to death the deeds of your sinful nature, you will live. For all
who are led by the Spirit of God are children of God.
ROMANS 8:12–14 NLT

Then Peter came to Jesus and asked, "Lord, how many times
shall I forgive my brother or sister who sins against me?
Up to seven times?" Jesus answered, "I tell you, not seven
times, but seventy-seven times."
MATTHEW 18:21–22 NIV

Righteousness exalts a nation,
but sin is a reproach to any people.
PROVERBS 14:34 NKJV

# 58

## Spiritual Fruit

Whether or not we expect to be, we are spiritual fruit producers. As we live day by day, others can see the love, faith, and goodness that flow from our lives as we serve Jesus. As we grow in Him, our lives testify to His greatness and the work He's doing in our lives.

But the fruit of the Spirit is love, joy, peace, longsuffering, kindness, goodness, faithfulness, gentleness, self-control. Against such there is no law.
GALATIANS 5:22–23 NKJV

Blessed is the one who does not walk in step with the wicked or stand in the way that sinners take or sit in the company of mockers, but whose delight is in the law of the LORD, and who meditates on his law day and night. That person is like a tree planted by streams of water, which yields its fruit in season and whose leaf does not wither—whatever they do prospers.
PSALM 1:1–3 NIV

Beware of false prophets who come disguised as harmless sheep but are really vicious wolves. You can identify them by their fruit, that is, by the way they act. Can you pick grapes from thornbushes, or figs from thistles? A good tree produces good fruit, and a bad tree produces bad fruit.
MATTHEW 7:15–17 NLT

> *God develops the fruit of the Spirit in your life by allowing you to experience circumstances in which you're tempted to express the exact opposite quality. Character development always involves a choice, and temptation provides that opportunity.*
> RICK WARREN

You did not choose me. I chose you and sent you out to produce fruit, the kind of fruit that will last. Then my Father will give you whatever you ask for in my name.
JOHN 15:16 CEV

Remain in me, as I also remain in you. No branch can bear fruit by itself; it must remain in the vine. Neither can you bear fruit unless you remain in me. I am the vine; you are the branches. If you remain in me and I in you, you will bear much fruit; apart from me you can do nothing. If you do not remain in me, you are like a branch that is thrown away and withers; such branches are picked up, thrown into the fire and burned.

JOHN 15:4–6 NIV

Likewise, my brothers, you also have died to the law through the body of Christ, so that you may belong to another, to him who has been raised from the dead, in order that we may bear fruit for God.

ROMANS 7:4 ESV

*The fruit of the Spirit is not push, drive, climb, grasp, and trample. . . .*
*Life is more than a climb to the top of the heap.*

RICHARD J. FOSTER

For you were once darkness, but now you are light in the Lord. Live as children of light (for the fruit of the light consists in all goodness, righteousness and truth) and find out what pleases the Lord.

EPHESIANS 5:8–10 NIV

*The Christian personality is hidden deep inside us. It is unseen,*
*like the soup carried in a tureen high over a waiter's head. No one*
*knows what's inside—unless the waiter is bumped and he trips!*
*Just so, people don't know what's inside us until we've been bumped.*
*But if Christ is living inside, what spills out is the fruit of the Spirit.*

HENRY WINGBLADE

# 59

## Spiritual Gifts

Did you know that you are a gifted person? God has given you a package of spiritual gifts that will take you a lifetime to unwrap. Your special combination of gifts is designed to suit the ministry God has in mind for you. Unwrap your gift today and make the most of it in His service!

But the manifestation of the Spirit is given to each one for the profit of all: for to one is given the word of wisdom through the Spirit, to another the word of knowledge through the same Spirit, to another faith by the same Spirit, to another gifts of healings by the same Spirit, to another the working of miracles, to another prophecy, to another discerning of spirits, to another different kinds of tongues, to another the interpretation of tongues. But one and the same Spirit works all these things, distributing to each one individually as He wills.

1 CORINTHIANS 12:7–11 NKJV

Now there are varieties of gifts, but the same Spirit.

1 CORINTHIANS 12:4–5 ESV

For I say, through the grace given to me, to everyone who is among you, not to think of himself more highly than he ought to think, but to think soberly, as God has dealt to each one a measure of faith. For as we have many members in one body, but all the members do not have the same function, so we, being many, are one body in Christ, and individually members of one another. Having then gifts differing according to the grace that is given to us, let us use them: if prophecy, let us prophesy in proportion to our faith; or ministry, let us use it in our ministering; he who teaches, in teaching; he who exhorts, in exhortation; he who gives, with liberality; he who leads, with diligence; he who shows mercy, with cheerfulness.

ROMANS 12:3–8 NKJV

And God placed in the church first of all apostles, second prophets, third teachers, then miracles, then gifts of healing, of helping, of guidance, and of different kinds of tongues.

1 CORINTHIANS 12:28 NIV

*Your spiritual gifts were not given for your own benefit but for the benefit of others, just as other people were given gifts for your benefit.*
RICK WARREN

So what makes us think we can escape if we ignore this great salvation that was first announced by the Lord Jesus himself and then delivered to us by those who heard him speak? And God confirmed the message by giving signs and wonders and various miracles and gifts of the Holy Spirit whenever he chose.
HEBREWS 2:3–4 NLT

*Do you have spiritual gifts and treasures that you have put into storage and are not using? Give them away; clear the closet!*
KATHERINE WALDEN

Pursue love, and earnestly desire the spiritual gifts, especially that you may prophesy.
1 CORINTHIANS 14:1 ESV

# 60

## Spiritual Refreshment

Some days spiritual dryness seems to fill our souls.
That's just when we need to seek Jesus for a time of
spiritual refreshment. A relationship with Him that
is growing closer will not remain dry too long.

For this is what the high and exalted One says—he who lives forever, whose name is holy: "I live in a high and holy place, but also with the one who is contrite and lowly in spirit, to revive the spirit of the lowly and to revive the heart of the contrite."
ISAIAH 57:15 NIV

*I drove away from my mind everything capable of spoiling the sense of the presence of God. . . . I just make it my business to persevere in His holy presence. . . . My soul has had an habitual, silent, secret conversation with God.*
BROTHER LAWRENCE

Therefore the people of Israel shall keep the Sabbath, observing the Sabbath throughout their generations, as a covenant forever. It is a sign forever between me and the people of Israel that in six days the LORD made heaven and earth, and on the seventh day he rested and was refreshed.
EXODUS 31:16–17 ESV

Trust in the LORD with all your heart, and lean not on your own understanding; in all your ways acknowledge Him, and He shall direct your paths. Do not be wise in your own eyes; fear the LORD and depart from evil. It will be health to your flesh, and strength to your bones.
PROVERBS 3:5–8 NKJV

*Revival is not just an emotional touch; it's a complete takeover!*
NANCY LEIGH DEMOSS

Repent, then, and turn to God, so that your sins may be wiped out, that times of refreshing may come from the Lord, and that he may send the Messiah, who has been appointed for you—even Jesus.
ACTS 3:19–20 NIV

# 61

## Success

The Bible often calls success "prosperity," and it describes not just earthly success but an effective spiritual life, too. Many times over, God promises to prosper His people if they obey His will.

Only be strong and very courageous; be careful to do according to all the law which Moses My servant commanded you; do not turn from it to the right or to the left, so that you may have success wherever you go. This book of the law shall not depart from your mouth, but you shall meditate on it day and night, so that you may be careful to do according to all that is written in it; for then you will make your way prosperous, and then you will have success.
JOSHUA 1:7–8 NASB

Therefore keep the words of this covenant and do them, that you may prosper in all that you do.
DEUTERONOMY 29:9 ESV

Blessed is the one who does not walk in step with the wicked or stand in the way that sinners take or sit in the company of mockers, but whose delight is in the law of the LORD, and who meditates on his law day and night. That person is like a tree planted by streams of water, which yields its fruit in season and whose leaf does not wither—whatever they do prospers.
PSALM 1:1–3 NIV

> *There are great positives as well as refusals necessary for him who would find real prosperity. He must not only say no to the wrong, he must say yes to the right. He must not only avoid the seat of the scornful, but his delight must be in the law of the Lord.*
> CLOVIS G. CHAPPELL

Who is the man who fears the LORD? He will instruct him in the way he should choose. His soul will abide in prosperity, and his descendants will inherit the land. The secret of the LORD is for those who fear Him, and He will make them know His covenant.
PSALM 25:12–14 NASB

The LORD was with Joseph so that he prospered, and he lived
in the house of his Egyptian master. When his master saw that
the LORD was with him and that the LORD gave him success in
everything he did, Joseph found favor in his eyes and became his
attendant. Potiphar put him in charge of his household, and he
entrusted to his care everything he owned.
GENESIS 39:2–4 NIV

David continued to succeed in everything he did,
for the LORD was with him.
1 SAMUEL 18:14 NLT

[King Hezekiah] trusted in the LORD, the God of Israel, so that
there was none like him among all the kings of Judah after
him, nor among those who were before him. For he held fast
to the LORD. He did not depart from following him, but kept the
commandments that the LORD commanded Moses. And the LORD
was with him; wherever he went out, he prospered. He rebelled
against the king of Assyria and would not serve him.
2 KINGS 18:5–7 ESV

*Before Nehemiah spoke to King Artaxerxes about rebuilding Jerusalem,*
*he prayed for success in bringing his case before the king. There is*
*nothing we cannot ask God for, as long as we are seeking His will.*

Lord, let your ear be attentive to the prayer of this your servant
and to the prayer of your servants who delight in revering your
name. Give your servant success today by granting him favor in
the presence of this man.
NEHEMIAH 1:11 NIV

Save now, I pray, O LORD; O LORD, I pray,
send now prosperity.
PSALM 118:25 NKJV

*Being humble involves the willingness to be
reckoned a failure in everyone's sight but God's.*
ROY M. PEARSON

Now in my prosperity I said, "I shall never be moved."
LORD, by Your favor You have made my mountain stand strong;
You hid Your face, and I was troubled.
PSALM 30:6–7 NKJV

*Faith is often strengthened right at the place of disappointment.*
RODNEY MCBRIDE

Enjoy prosperity while you can, but when hard times strike,
realize that both come from God. Remember that nothing is
certain in this life.
ECCLESIASTES 7:14 NLT

Terrors are turned against me; they pursue my honor as the wind,
and my prosperity has passed away like a cloud.
JOB 30:15 NASB

Rest in the LORD, and wait patiently for Him;
do not fret because of him who prospers in his way,
because of the man who brings wicked schemes to pass.
PSALM 37:7 NKJV

# 62

*Suicide*

Though the Bible includes a number of stories of
suicides, it never approves of the act, which breaks
the sixth commandment. Those who kill themselves
or ask others to kill them, in these examples,
were at odds with God, not fervent believers.

Thou shalt not kill.
DEUTERONOMY 5:17 KJV

Today I have given you the choice between life and death,
between blessings and curses. Now I call on heaven and
earth to witness the choice you make. Oh, that you would
choose life, so that you and your descendants might live!
DEUTERONOMY 30:19 NLT

> *The way we view death determines, to a*
> *surprising degree, the way we live our lives.*
> BILLY GRAHAM

But a certain woman threw an upper millstone on Abimelech's
head, crushing his skull. Then he called quickly to the young man,
his armor bearer, and said to him, "Draw your sword and kill me,
so that it will not be said of me, 'A woman slew him.'" So the
young man pierced him through, and he died.
JUDGES 9:53–54 NASB

Then Samson put his hands on the two center pillars that held
up the temple. Pushing against them with both hands, he prayed,
"Let me die with the Philistines." And the temple crashed down
on the Philistine rulers and all the people. So he killed more
people when he died than he had during his entire lifetime.
JUDGES 16:29–30 NLT

Then Judas threw the silver coins down in the Temple and went
out and hanged himself.
MATTHEW 27:5 NLT

Then Saul said to his armorbearer, "Draw your sword, and thrust me through with it, lest these uncircumcised men come and thrust me through and abuse me." But his armorbearer would not, for he was greatly afraid. Therefore Saul took a sword and fell on it. And when his armorbearer saw that Saul was dead, he also fell on his sword, and died with him.
1 Samuel 31:4–5 NKJV

> *It is when a man has no one to love him that he commits suicide.*
> *So long as he has friends, those who love him and whom*
> *he loves, he will live, because to live is to love.*
> Henry Drummond

When Ahithophel saw that his advice had not been followed, he saddled his donkey and set out for his house in his hometown. He put his house in order and then hanged himself. So he died and was buried in his father's tomb.
2 Samuel 17:23 NIV

When Zimri saw that the city was taken, he went into the citadel of the royal palace and set the palace on fire around him. So he died, because of the sins he had committed, doing evil in the eyes of the LORD and following the ways of Jeroboam and committing the same sin Jeroboam had caused Israel to commit.
1 Kings 16:18–19 NIV

> *No man must let the tenant out of the*
> *tenement till God the landlord calls for it.*
> Thomas Adams

# 63
## Temptation

All of us experience temptations in various forms. God has wise advice concerning those things that would lead us into sin: Flee from them! If we do not sit around waiting for sin to knock on our doors, how much of it could we avoid?

Don't blame God when you are tempted! God cannot be tempted
by evil, and he doesn't use evil to tempt others. We are tempted
by our own desires that drag us off and trap us. Our desires
make us sin, and when sin is finished with us, it leaves us dead.
JAMES 1:13–15 CEV

Because [Jesus] himself suffered when he was tempted,
he is able to help those who are being tempted.
HEBREWS 2:18 NIV

This High Priest of ours understands our weaknesses,
for he faced all of the same testings we do, yet he did not sin.
HEBREWS 4:15 NLT

*If we do not abide in prayer, we will abide in temptation.*
JOHN OWEN

Lead us not into temptation, but deliver us from the evil one.
MATTHEW 6:13 NIV

Watch and pray, lest you enter into temptation.
The spirit indeed is willing, but the flesh is weak.
MATTHEW 26:41 NKJV

*I cannot tell how I am buffeted sometimes by temptation. I never knew
how bad a heart I have. Yet I do know that I love God and love His
work, and desire to serve Him only and in all things. And I value
above all else that precious Savior in whom alone I can be accepted.*
JAMES HUDSON TAYLOR

No temptation has overtaken you except what is common to mankind. And God is faithful; he will not let you be tempted beyond what you can bear. But when you are tempted, he will also provide a way out so that you can endure it.
1 CORINTHIANS 10:13 NIV

Brethren, even if anyone is caught in any trespass, you who are spiritual, restore such a one in a spirit of gentleness; each one looking to yourself, so that you too will not be tempted.
GALATIANS 6:1 NASB

But those who desire to be rich fall into temptation, into a snare, into many senseless and harmful desires that plunge people into ruin and destruction.
1 TIMOTHY 6:9 ESV

> *Temptations, when we meet them at first, are as the lion that reared upon Samson; but if we overcome them, the next time we see them we shall find a nest of honey within them.*
> JOHN BUNYAN

Consider it a sheer gift, friends, when tests and challenges come at you from all sides. You know that under pressure, your faith-life is forced into the open and shows its true colors. So don't try to get out of anything prematurely. Let it do its work so you become mature and well-developed, not deficient in any way.
JAMES 1:2 MSG

Submit therefore to God. Resist the devil
and he will flee from you.
JAMES 4:7 NASB

Blessed is the one who perseveres under trial, because, having stood the test, that person will receive the crown of life that the Lord has promised to those who love him. When tempted, no one should say, "God is tempting me." For God cannot be tempted by evil, nor does he tempt anyone; but each person is tempted when they are dragged away by their own evil desire and enticed.
JAMES 1:12–14 NIV

> *The Bible teaches us in times of temptation. . .there is one command: Flee! Get away from it. . .for every struggle against lust in one's own strength is doomed to failure.*
> DIETRICH BONHOEFFER

Run from temptations that capture young people. Always do the right thing. Be faithful, loving, and easy to get along with. Worship with people whose hearts are pure.
2 TIMOTHY 2:22 CEV

Flee from sexual immorality. All other sins a person commits are outside the body, but whoever sins sexually, sins against their own body.
1 CORINTHIANS 6:18 NIV

Do not deprive each other of sexual relations, unless you both agree to refrain from sexual intimacy for a limited time so you can give yourselves more completely to prayer. Afterward, you should come together again so that Satan won't be able to tempt you because of your lack of self-control.
1 CORINTHIANS 7:5 NLT

# 64

## Terrorism

We may remember a time when terrorism was a word for other nations. We lived in a land largely untouched by the violence and danger of others. But today terrorism is a real fear that often threatens to overwhelm us. No matter what we experience, nothing is larger than God. He protects and encourages us, just as He calls the terrorist to give up his ways and turn instead to Him. As a people turn their hearts toward the living God, vengeance disappears.

Thou shalt not kill.
EXODUS 20:13 KJV

*Those who experience the damages of terrorism can
also be certain that God has not forgotten them.
He is the just Judge who does not excuse terrorists' actions.*

The LORD passed in front of Moses, calling out, "Yahweh!
The Lord! The God of compassion and mercy! I am slow to anger
and filled with unfailing love and faithfulness. I lavish unfailing
love to a thousand generations. I forgive iniquity, rebellion, and
sin. But I do not excuse the guilty. I lay the sins of the parents
upon their children and grandchildren; the entire family is
affected—even children in the third and fourth generations."
EXODUS 34:6–7 NLT

Dearly beloved, avenge not yourselves, but rather give place unto
wrath: for it is written, Vengeance is mine; I will repay, saith the Lord.
ROMANS 12:19 KJV

*Ultimately, God is the One who will right all wrongs. Vengeance
is lawlessness because it does not recognize the lawful and righteous
execution of God's judgment which He will bring about in His time.*
LOU PRIOLO

The LORD trieth the righteous: but the wicked
and him that loveth violence his soul hateth.
PSALM 11:5 KJV

*We fear men so much, because we fear God so little.
One fear cures another. When man's terror scares you,
turn your thoughts to the wrath of God.*
WILLIAM GURNALL

Do not be afraid of those who kill the body but
cannot kill the soul. Rather, be afraid of the One
who can destroy both soul and body in hell.
MATTHEW 10:28 NIV

If someone kidnaps a person, the penalty is death, regardless of
whether the person has been sold or is still held in possession.
EXODUS 21:16 MSG

If a man is found kidnapping any of his brethren of the children
of Israel, and mistreats him or sells him, then that kidnapper shall
die; and you shall put away the evil from among you.
DEUTERONOMY 24:7 NKJV

This is what the LORD says: Be fair-minded and just. Do what
is right. . . . Quit your evil deeds! Do not mistreat foreigners,
orphans, and widows. Stop murdering the innocent!
JEREMIAH 22:3 NLT

*The terrible thing about terrorism is that
ultimately it destroys those who practice it.*
TERRY WAITE

A murderer's tormented conscience will drive him
into the grave. Don't protect him!
PROVERBS 28:17 NLT

*The most dangerous spiritual violence is that which
carries our will away with a false enthusiasm which seems
to come from God but which is in reality inspired by passion.*
THOMAS MERTON

Blessings are on the head of the righteous,
but violence covers the mouth of the wicked.
PROVERBS 10:6 NKJV


A man shall eat well by the fruit of his mouth,
but the soul of the unfaithful feeds on violence.
PROVERBS 13:2 NKJV


> *What a cruel thing war is. . .to fill our hearts*
> *with hatred instead of love for our neighbors.*
> ROBERT E. LEE


The wicked will go down to the grave.
This is the fate of all the nations who ignore God.
PSALM 9:17 NLT


In his arrogance the wicked man hunts down the weak,
who are caught in the schemes he devises.
PSALM 10:2 NIV


The God of my rock; in him will I trust: he is my shield,
and the horn of my salvation, my high tower, and my refuge,
my savior; thou savest me from violence.
2 SAMUEL 22:3 KJV


He will cover you with his feathers, and under his wings you will
find refuge; his faithfulness will be your shield and rampart.
You will not fear the terror of night, nor the arrow that flies by day.
PSALM 91:4–6 NIV

# 65

## The Poor

Contrary to popular belief, the poor have not been deserted by God. He often uses people to help supply the impoverished person's needs and calls on Christians to aid those who lack money. Yet our Lord also warns against behavior that leads to poverty and encourages believers to give their best to their work.

Give generously to the poor, not grudgingly, for the LORD your God will bless you in everything you do. There will always be some in the land who are poor. That is why I am commanding you to share freely with the poor.

DEUTERONOMY 15:10–11 NLT

Do not take advantage of a hired worker who is poor and needy, whether that worker is a fellow Israelite or a foreigner residing in one of your towns.

DEUTERONOMY 24:14 NIV

*Give according to your income, lest God make your income according to your giving.*

OSWALD J. SMITH

The LORD makes some poor and others rich; he brings some down and lifts others up. He lifts the poor from the dust and the needy from the garbage dump. He sets them among princes, placing them in seats of honor. For all the earth is the LORD's, and he has set the world in order.

1 SAMUEL 2:7–8 NLT

For He will deliver the needy when he cries, the poor also, and him who has no helper. He will spare the poor and needy, and will save the souls of the needy. He will redeem their life from oppression and violence; and precious shall be their blood in His sight.

PSALM 72:12–14 NKJV

*Though poor in this world's goods, though grieving the loss of loved ones, though suffering pain of body, though harassed by sin and Satan, though hated and persecuted by worldlings, whatever be the case and lot of the Christian, it is both his privilege and duty to rejoice in the Lord.*

A. W. PINK

Then Jesus turned to his disciples and said, "God blesses you who are poor, for the Kingdom of God is yours. God blesses you who are hungry now, for you will be satisfied. God blesses you who weep now, for in due time you will laugh. What blessings await you when people hate you and exclude you and mock you and curse you as evil because you follow the Son of Man. When that happens, be happy! Yes, leap for joy! For a great reward awaits you in heaven. And remember, their ancestors treated the ancient prophets that same way.
LUKE 6:20–23 NLT

*Of all God's creatures, man alone is poor.*
JANE WELSH CARLYLE

My little group of disciples, don't be afraid! Your Father wants to give you the kingdom. Sell what you have and give the money to the poor. Make yourselves moneybags that never wear out. Make sure your treasure is safe in heaven, where thieves cannot steal it and moths cannot destroy it.
LUKE 12:32–33 CEV

You who seek God, let your hearts revive. For the LORD hears the needy and does not despise his own people who are prisoners.
PSALM 69:32–33 ESV

*The poor man's hand is the treasury of Christ.*
HENRY ALFORD

The generous will themselves be blessed,
for they share their food with the poor.
PROVERBS 22:9 NIV

Each of you should give what you have decided in your heart to give, not reluctantly or under compulsion, for God loves a cheerful giver. And God is able to bless you abundantly, so that in all things at all times, having all that you need, you will abound in every good work. As it is written: "They have freely scattered their gifts to the poor; their righteousness endures forever."
2 CORINTHIANS 9:7–9 NIV

Those who give to the poor will lack nothing, but those who close their eyes to them receive many curses.
PROVERBS 28:27 NIV

Jesus answered, "If you want to be perfect, go, sell your possessions and give to the poor, and you will have treasure in heaven. Then come, follow me." When the young man heard this, he went away sad, because he had great wealth. Then Jesus said to his disciples, "I tell you the truth, it is hard for someone who is rich to enter the kingdom of heaven. Again I tell you, it is easier for a camel to go through the eye of a needle than for someone who is rich to enter the kingdom of God."
MATTHEW 19:21–24 NIV

But Zacchaeus stood up and said to the Lord, "Look, Lord! Here and now I give half of my possessions to the poor, and if I have cheated anybody out of anything, I will pay back four times the amount."
LUKE 19:8 NIV

The rich ruleth over the poor,
and the borrower is servant to the lender.
PROVERBS 22:7 KJV

The poor are despised even by their neighbors,
while the rich have many "friends."
PROVERBS 14:20 NLT

This is what the LORD Almighty said: "Administer true justice;
show mercy and compassion to one another. Do not oppress
the widow or the fatherless, the foreigner or the poor.
Do not plot evil against each other."
ZECHARIAH 7:8–10 NIV

*A double standard for justice that denies it to the poor is
nothing new in this world. God warned against this
in His Law, and we still struggle against it today.*

Do not deny justice to your poor people in their lawsuits.
EXODUS 23:6 NIV

You shall do no injustice in judgment; you shall
not be partial to the poor nor defer to the great,
but you are to judge your neighbor fairly.
LEVITICUS 19:15 NASB

The righteous care about justice for the poor,
but the wicked have no such concern.
PROVERBS 29:7 NIV

He who oppresses the poor to make more for himself
or who gives to the rich, will only come to poverty.
PROVERBS 22:16 NASB

*Those who would bring great things to pass must rise early.*
*Love not sleep, lest thou come to poverty.*
MATTHEW HENRY

Good planning and hard work lead to prosperity,
but hasty shortcuts lead to poverty.
PROVERBS 21:5 NLT

Poverty and shame will come to him who neglects discipline,
but he who regards reproof will be honored.
PROVERBS 13:18 NASB

In all labor there is profit, but idle chatter leads only to poverty.
PROVERBS 14:23 NKJV

A hard worker has plenty of food,
but a person who chases fantasies ends up in poverty.
PROVERBS 28:19 NLT

Do not join those who drink too much wine or gorge
themselves on meat, for drunkards and gluttons
become poor, and drowsiness clothes them in rags.
PROVERBS 23:20–21 NIV

*As covetousness is the root of all evil,*
*so poverty is the worst of all snares.*
DANIEL DEFOE

The rich man's wealth is his fortress,
the ruin of the poor is their poverty.
PROVERBS 10:15 NASB

# 66

## Tolerance

Scripture does not tell Christians to condone the
modern idea of tolerance, which accepts any ideas and
rarely confronts another's beliefs; we cannot simply
ignore the differences between ourselves and those who
do not believe. God commands us to share the gospel.
But He also calls us to a higher standard than tolerance.
We are to love all others, from fellow Christians to our
enemies, and to seek unity with our fellow believers.

For God so loved the world, that he gave his only begotten
Son, that whosoever believeth in him should not perish, but
have everlasting life. For God sent not his Son into the world
to condemn the world; but that the world through him might
be saved. He that believeth on him is not condemned: but he
that believeth not is condemned already, because he hath not
believed in the name of the only begotten Son of God.
JOHN 3:16–18 KJV

*Tolerance is the virtue of the man without convictions.*
G. K. CHESTERTON

And this gospel of the kingdom will be preached in the whole
world as a testimony to all nations, and then the end will come.
MATTHEW 24:14 NIV

For I am not ashamed of the gospel, for it is the power
of God for salvation to everyone who believes, to the
Jew first and also to the Greek.
ROMANS 1:16 ESV

*In the world it is called Tolerance, but in hell it is called*
*Despair, the sin that believes in nothing, cares for nothing,*
*seeks to know nothing, interferes with nothing, enjoys nothing,*
*hates nothing, finds purpose in nothing, lives for nothing,*
*and remains alive because there is nothing for which it will die.*
DOROTHY SAYERS

A new command I give you: Love one another.
As I have loved you, so you must love one another.
JOHN 13:34 NIV

But I tell you: Love your enemies and pray
for those who persecute you, that you may
be children of your Father in heaven.
MATTHEW 5:44–45 NIV

Beloved, if God so loved us, we also ought to love one another.
1 JOHN 4:11 NKJV

Love each other with genuine affection,
and take delight in honoring each other.
ROMANS 12:10 NLT

*Use God's Word, not what people around you are willing to accept,*
*to set the standards for what is right or wrong.*
BRUCE BARTON

Walk worthy of the calling with which you were called,
with all lowliness and gentleness, with longsuffering,
bearing with one another in love, endeavoring to keep
the unity of the Spirit in the bond of peace.
EPHESIANS 4:1–3 NKJV

Therefore let us not judge one another anymore,
but rather determine this—not to put an obstacle
or a stumbling block in a brother's way.
ROMANS 14:13 NASB

Be kind to one another, tenderhearted, forgiving one another,
as God in Christ forgave you.
EPHESIANS 4:32 ESV

# 67

## Trust

Trust is key to any relationship——between parent and child, between friends, certainly between a husband and wife. And trust is the cornerstone of our relationship with God as well. Over and over, the Bible tells us to "trust in the Lord." If we can't trust Him, who can we trust?

"Do not put your trust in idols or make metal images
of gods for yourselves. I am the LORD your God."
LEVITICUS 19:4 NLT

The LORD is a shelter for the oppressed, a refuge in times of
trouble. Those who know your name trust in you, for you,
O LORD, do not abandon those who search for you.
PSALM 9:9–10 NLT

The instructions of the LORD are perfect, reviving the soul.
The decrees of the LORD are trustworthy, making wise the simple.
PSALM 19:7 NLT

Even strong young lions sometimes go hungry,
but those who trust in the LORD will lack no good thing.
PSALM 34:10 NLT

Christ will make his home in your hearts as you trust in him.
Your roots will grow down into God's love and keep you strong.
EPHESIANS 3:17 NLT

The LORD is my strength and my shield; in him my heart trusts,
and I am helped; my heart exults, and with my song
I give thanks to him.
PSALM 28:7 ESV

Many are the woes of the wicked, but the LORD's
unfailing love surrounds the one who trusts in him.
PSALM 32:10 NIV

Commit your way to the LORD, trust also in Him,
and He shall bring it to pass.
PSALM 37:5 NKJV

*Talk what we will of faith, if we do not trust*
*and rely upon Him, we do not believe in Him.*
ANTONY FARINDON

I will not trust in my bow, nor will my sword save me.
But You have saved us from our adversaries, and You have
put to shame those who hate us.
PSALM 44:6–7 NASB

Whenever I am afraid, I will trust in You.
PSALM 56:3 NKJV

*The creeping wilderness will soon take over that church*
*that trusts in its own strength and forgets to watch and pray.*
A. W. TOZER

I will say of the LORD, "He is my refuge
and my fortress, my God, in whom I trust."
PSALM 91:2 NIV

Bad news won't bother [those who fear the Lord];
they have decided to trust the LORD.
PSALM 112:7 CEV

It is better to take refuge in the LORD than to trust in man.
PSALM 118:8 NASB

# 68

## Unbelief

We all face decisions about whether or not to trust God. But the struggle to avoid unbelief is worth it all when we see the benefits of trusting Jesus and experience His love.

Abraham never wavered in believing God's promise. In fact, his faith grew stronger, and in this he brought glory to God. He was fully convinced that God is able to do whatever he promises.
ROMANS 4:20–21 NLT

Again and again the LORD had sent his prophets and seers to warn both Israel and Judah: "Turn from all your evil ways. . . . " But the Israelites would not listen. They were as stubborn as their ancestors who had refused to believe in the LORD their God. They rejected his decrees and the covenant he had made with their ancestors, and they despised all his warnings. They worshiped worthless idols, so they became worthless themselves.
2 KINGS 17:13–15 NLT

*Such as do not grow in grace, decay in grace. There is no standing at a stay in religion, either we go forward or backward; if faith doth not grow, unbelief will; if heavenly mindedness doth not grow, covetousness will. A man that doth not increase his stock diminisheth it; if you do not improve your stock of grace, your stock will decay.*
THOMAS WATSON

Today, if you hear his voice, do not harden your hearts as you did in the rebellion, during the time of testing in the wilderness, where your ancestors tested and tried me, though for forty years they saw what I did. That is why I was angry with that generation; I said, "Their hearts are always going astray, and they have not known my ways."
HEBREWS 3:7–10 NIV

And to whom did God swear that they would never enter his rest if not to those who disobeyed? So we see that [the Jews] were not able to enter, because of their unbelief.
HEBREWS 3:18–19 NIV

All who have raged against [God] will be brought before him,
disgraced by their unbelief. And all who are connected
with Israel will have a robust, praising, good life in God!
ISAIAH 45:24 MSG

But although He had done so many signs before them, [the Jews]
did not believe in Him, that the word of Isaiah the prophet might
be fulfilled, which he spoke: "Lord, who has believed our report?
And to whom has the arm of the Lord been revealed?"
JOHN 12:37–38 NKJV

*Only look to Jesus. He died for you, died in your place, died under
the frowns of heaven, that we might die under its smile. Regard neither
unbelief nor doubt. Fear neither sin nor hell. Choose neither life nor
death. All these are swallowed up in the immensity of Christ and are
triumphed over in His cross.*
JOHN FLETCHER

"If you can'?" said Jesus. "Everything is possible for one
who believes." Immediately the boy's father exclaimed,
"I do believe; help me overcome my unbelief!"
MARK 9:23–24 NIV

Still later, as the Eleven were eating supper, he appeared and
took them to task most severely for their stubborn unbelief,
refusing to believe those who had seen him raised up.
MARK 16:14 MSG

*The curse, of this age especially, is unbelief, frittering the real meaning
of God's Word away, and making it all figure and fiction.*
CATHERINE BOOTH

# 69
## Wisdom

Wisdom comes from God, not people. But those who
walk closely with Him can be good advisors when we
need help. No one should avoid getting good advice
when it's needed, and going first to God, then to
godly humans, will lead us into wise decisions.

Oh, the depth of the riches both of the wisdom and knowledge of God! How unsearchable are His judgments and His ways past finding out!
ROMANS 11:33 NKJV

No wisdom, no understanding, no counsel
can avail against the LORD.
PROVERBS 21:30 ESV

*Wisdom [is] an understanding and application*
*of the moral principles of God.*
JERRY BRIDGES

The fear of the LORD is the beginning of wisdom: and the knowledge of the holy is understanding.
PROVERBS 9:10 KJV

How blessed is the man who finds wisdom and the man who gains understanding. For her profit is better than the profit of silver and her gain better than fine gold.
PROVERBS 3:13–14 NASB

*A truly humble man is sensible of his natural distance from God. . .*
*of the insufficiency of his own power and wisdom. . .and that he needs*
*God's wisdom to lead and guide him, and His might to enable*
*him to do what he ought to do for Him.*
JONATHAN EDWARDS

Don't be impressed with your own wisdom. Instead, fear the LORD and turn away from evil.
PROVERBS 3:7 NLT

If you need wisdom, ask our generous God, and he will give it to you. He will not rebuke you for asking.
JAMES 1:5 NLT

*There is nothing more foolish than an act of wickedness;*
*there is no wisdom equal to that of obeying God.*
ALBERT BARNES

Wisdom will protect you from the smooth talk of a sinful woman, who breaks her wedding vows and leaves the man she married when she was young.
PROVERBS 2:16–17 CEV

Where there is strife, there is pride,
but wisdom is found in those who take advice.
PROVERBS 13:10 NIV

Listen to advice and accept instruction,
that you may gain wisdom in the future.
PROVERBS 19:20 ESV

Wisdom is more precious than rubies,
and nothing you desire can compare with her.
PROVERBS 8:11 NIV

Who is wise and understanding among you?
Let them show it by their good life, by deeds
done in the humility that comes from wisdom.
JAMES 3:13 NIV

# 70

## Worry

God knows that worries can easily overwhelm us. That's why He tells us not to worry and encourages us to trust in Him. When our concerns are in His hands, they are in the right place.

Cast all your anxiety on him because he cares for you.
1 PETER 5:7 NIV

Don't fret or worry. Instead of worrying, pray. Let petitions and praises shape your worries into prayers, letting God know your concerns. Before you know it, a sense of God's wholeness, everything coming together for good, will come and settle you down. It's wonderful what happens when Christ displaces worry at the center of your life.
PHILIPPIANS 4:6 MSG

Therefore I tell you, do not worry about your life, what you will eat or drink; or about your body, what you will wear. Is not life more than food, and the body more than clothes?
MATTHEW 6:25 NIV

*God never built a Christian strong enough to carry today's duties and tomorrow's anxieties piled on top of them.*
THEODORE LEDYARD CUYLER

And who of you by being worried can add a single hour to his life?
MATTHEW 6:27 NASB

Do not be anxious, saying, "What shall we eat?" or "What shall we drink?" or "What shall we wear?"
MATTHEW 6:31 ESV

*Worry does not empty tomorrow of its sorrow.*
*It empties today of its strength.*
CORRIE TEN BOOM

Do not worry about tomorrow, for tomorrow will worry about itself. Each day has enough trouble of its own.
MATTHEW 6:34 NIV

*The strong hands of God twisted the crown of thorns into a crown of glory; and in such hands we are safe.*
CHARLES WILLIAMS

You will stand trial before governors and kings because you are my followers. But this will be your opportunity to tell the rulers and other unbelievers about me. When you are arrested, don't worry about how to respond or what to say. God will give you the right words at the right time. For it is not you who will be speaking—it will be the Spirit of your Father speaking through you.
MATTHEW 10:18–20 NLT

*Every evening I turn my worries over to God. He's going to be up all night anyway.*
MARY C. CROWLEY

When my anxious thoughts multiply within me,
Your consolations delight my soul.
PSALM 94:19 NASB

Search me, O God, and know my heart;
test me and know my anxious thoughts.
PSALM 139:23 NIV

Anxiety in the heart of man causes depression,
but a good word makes it glad.
PROVERBS 12:25 NKJV